PICKLED

Published by

Adams Media, a division of F+W Media, Inc.

57 Littlefield Street, Avon, MA 02322. U.S.A.

www.adamsmedia.com

ISBN 10: 1-4405-3873-5

ISBN 13: 978-1-4405-3873-5

eISBN 10: 1-4405-4023-3

eISBN 13: 978-1-4405-4023-3

Printed in China.

10   9   8   7   6   5   4   3   2   1

Library of Congress Cataloging-in-Publication Data
is available from the publisher.

This publication is designed to provide accurate and authoritative information with regard to the subject matter
covered. It is sold with the understanding that the publisher is not engaged in rendering legal, accounting, or
other professional advice. If legal advice or other expert assistance is required, the services of a competent
professional person should be sought.

—From a *Declaration of Principles* jointly adopted by a Committee of the American Bar Association
and a Committee of Publishers and Associations

Photos pages 4, 8, 10, 21, 30, 32, 40, 43–45, 48, 51, 54, 56, 59, 63, 82, 84, 88, 90, 119, 122, 127, 130, 133

© www.stockfood.com, pages 13, 35, 39, 47, 77, 96, 99, 105, 108, 114 © www.istockphoto.com,

pages 17, 18, 23, 24, 66, 74, 134, 137 © www.123rf.com, page 15 © www.clipart.com.

This book is available at quantity discounts for bulk purchases. For information, please call 1-800-289-0963.

PICKLED

From **CURING LEMONS** to **FERMENTING CABBAGE**,
the gourmand's ultimate guide to the world of pickling

❦ KELLY CARROLATA ❧

-100-
Tangy, Sweet,
Juicy, Crunchy,
Salty Recipes . . .
to Relish

▲ **adams**media
Avon, Massachusetts

Pickled Peaches, see Part II

CONTENTS

PART III
MEALS with PICKLES 97

PART IV

DRINKS with PICKLES 135

Nasturtium, see Part II

INTRODUCTION

Decadent, sophisticated, adventurous . . . are these really words that can be used to describe the humble pickle? Absolutely! Once a simple survival skill, pickling is now the trendiest food movement around, valued across the culinary world for its ability to take ordinary ingredients—vegetables, fruits, and even meats— and almost magically imbue them with remarkably vibrant flavor. But today's upscale fermenting is not the exclusive domain of the four-star chef. With just a handful of simple, fresh ingredients and a few techniques, anyone can produce delicious amuse-bouches, entrées, and even pickled cocktails that push the envelope of epicurean innovation.

With creations that run the gamut from a sophisticated and quirky Prime Rib with Quick-Pickled Ramp Aioli to classic Heirloom Mustard Pickles, you can ease into the world of fermented foods by being as highbrow or as lowbrow as you like. There are no rules when it comes to enjoying your pickles! And since today's hippest pickled foods are often as simple as they are sophisticated, it's easy to start turning out easy recipes that still deliver an exciting culinary payoff.

In Part I of this book, you'll learn the mechanics of pickling, including important concerns of preparation and safety, so that you're ready to get down to the business of pickling in your own kitchen. You'll see what separates pickles from other types of preserved foods, and what makes them such a culinary powerhouse. Then Parts II, III, and IV will broaden your home-cooking horizons as we dish out nearly a hundred upscale—yet accessible—recipes that take you from your first cucumber all the way to dinner party fare, and hyper-cool pickled cocktails for the truly adventurous gourmand.

From the picnic table to the pinnacle of haute cuisine, whether you're cooking pub grub or setting up a once-in-a-lifetime soiree, you'll find exactly what you need in the recipes and techniques contained here. Regardless of whether you consider yourself a DIY enthusiast or a member of the culinary elite, you should never be afraid to experiment with your pickles—great food is all about balancing unexpected contrasting flavors and textures, so be sure to have some fun with your cutting-edge creations and let the bold new ingredients here take center stage. It's time to hit the farmers' market, grab some glass jars, and jump in to the hip world of pickling!

PART I

HOW
TO
PICKLE

Crisp pickled vegetables, nuanced preserved fruits, and piquant relishes and chutneys: these once-humble pickles have become the foundation of a new generation of home DIY enthusiasts and gourmet chefs alike, a culinary art form that is as at home in the pantry as it is in a four-star restaurant. As high-end as pickled ingredients have come to be, pickling itself has been refined over thousands of years and is not a difficult process, once you have a firm grasp of a few basic techniques! In this section, you'll get a brief history of pickling as a preservation method, and then you'll learn the four primary styles of pickles, general steps for safely preserving your produce, and how to go about canning or jarring your pickles for long-term storage and enjoyment. If you're ever unclear or unsure about how to handle a recipe, the helpful guidelines presented here should offer everything you need to safely and consistently create deliciously upscale pickles. And once you've got the culinary basics under your belt, the recipes will be a breeze!

The Peculiar History of PICKLES

When you pickle, you are not only creating a vibrant, gourmet ingredient, but you are also reenacting a process that has been practiced and perfected over many thousands of years, by cultures all over the planet. Pickling has been around, in one form or another, for more than 4,000 years. The first archaeological evidence of pickles comes from ancient Mesopotamia and the Tigris River valley, from nearly 3,000 B.C.E. From then, they never faded out of fashion, with pickles appearing in the writings of Aristotle and in the Bible. They were also associated with famous leaders such as Julius Caesar and Cleopatra, both of whom believed pickles possessed semi-miraculous qualities as an aid to spiritual and physical well-being. Pickles were a widely enjoyed snack during the Middle Ages in Europe, and they quickly became among the most popular preserving methods for sailors, both because pickles would stay fresh for the duration of the voyage, and because

they helped prevent scurvy. Amerigo Vespucci, the namesake of America, was a pickle merchant before he was an explorer and mapmaker. Pickles became such a large part of popular culture that even Christopher Columbus grew cucumbers in the Caribbean for the express purpose of making pickles. Think of that the next time you're toiling in your garden with a stubborn cucumber plant!

In the mid-eighteenth century, Napoleon Bonaparte offered a $250,000 bounty for anyone who could work out a technique to safely preserve pickles and other foods for his armies over long durations. In response, Nicholas Appert discovered that food wouldn't spoil if it was placed in an airtight jar and then boiled, thus giving birth to the modern invention of canning, and allowing for a variety of nonfermented pickles to be stored for longer periods of time. For the past two centuries, the technology of pickling has remained pretty much the same, even as the taste and prevalence of pickles changed. Today, pickles are a full-blown obsession among chefs, growers, and foodies alike—"Pickle Day" is now a yearly celebration, and the average American consumes nine pounds of pickles annually. It's hard to blame us, though: Pickles are piquant, healthy, long-lasting, and, best of all, they're easy to make and even easier to cook with. And because pickling methods have been refined for thousands of years, it's easy, once the basics are learned, to focus on experimenting with more and more inventive and memorable pickle flavors. Gourmet restaurants all over the country now employ pickled ingredients in a variety of delicious dishes, and it's never been easier for at-home chefs to do the same.

SWEET Techniques and SALTY Science

Making a pickle is so deceptively simple that you won't believe the incredible changes that happen in your vegetables—until you taste them, that is! Basically, pickling is the process of preserving food by making it acidic, which helps prevent the growth of bacteria and delays spoilage. Usually, you'll submerge your food in a brine that's made either with just salt and water, or with vinegar. You'll probably also want to add some layers of flavor to your pickles, so most brines also get a healthy dose of dill, garlic, allspice, clove, or other spices. From here, you'll sometimes want to can your pickled vegetables for long-term storage, but other times you might want to eat them straight away, tossing them into a composed salad or topping a sandwich with them.

The beauty of pickling is that knowing just a few simple techniques like fermenting, brining, and canning gives you a world of culinary options for your pickles. For instance, the same item can usually be pickled in at least four different ways, all of which we'll be exploring here! The first typical technique is fresh-pack (also known as quick-process), which utilizes vinegar of at least 5 percent strength to create the acidic medium for your pickles. These types of pickles are the quickest, easiest, and safest to create, and they make up the bulk of the recipes in this book. If you're feeling more traditional, you could opt for fermentation, generally used for sauerkraut, kimchi, and old-fashioned dill pickles. In fermented pickles, the acid is created by natural lactobacteria (a good bacteria) that form while your pickle sits under a salty brine. The third general pickling method is that of the fruit pickle, which is generally topped with a boiling sugar-vinegar syrup that will give your pickles a complex sweet-sour flavor, perfect for upscale desserts or avant-garde savory courses. The last common pickle technique is chutney and relish, whereby fruits or vegetables are generally chopped and then cooked down in

a strong vinegar solution. Chutneys and relishes are delectable sides to strongly flavored ethnic cuisines, especially Indian and Malaysian.

No matter what type of pickle you want to serve (and preserve), always start with garden-fresh fruits or vegetables, fresh spices, and clean water. Try to get your produce at a trustworthy farmers' market, or grow it yourself if you've got a green thumb. If you're harvesting your own fruits and vegetables, do so early in the morning and refrigerate them immediately, before preparing all your pickling equipment. And whichever type of pickle you want to make, be sure that you follow your recipe to the letter—ratios of salt and acid are very important to safety in pickling, and this isn't the time for experimentation! If something is too tart for your taste buds, add a pinch of sugar or a dollop of honey to mellow it out, but don't dilute the vinegar or brine.

Classic Fermented Pickles

These pickles have the most cachet among DIYers, because they're the most traditional of all pickles, and they last the longest in storage. They can also be the most intimidating, though, since most cooks don't have experience with home fermentation. Don't let that dissuade you—the deep and complex flavors that fermentation produces are a culinary payoff that's well worth the attention you'll need to give to your pickles.

To ferment a traditional pickle, you'll need to whip up some basic pickling brine at a ratio of 1 quart water to ½ cup pickling salt—and don't be afraid to add some classic spices like dill and garlic to your taste. The container that

with rocks or some other implement, depending on the size and shape of your container. In all cases, the brine should cover the pickles by at least 1 inch. Your entire crock or jar should then be covered in either a loose lid, or a breathable barrier like a coffee filter or some tea towels.

At room temperature, it takes about a month for a whole cucumber pickle to be completely fermented, with other vegetables clocking in at slightly less time. Don't just put your pickles in the fermenting crock and then forget about them, though! You should check your fermenting pickles every day to make sure that they're fully submerged. Over time, you'll likely notice mold on the surface of your mixture—this is normal, and you can remove it with a clean, washed spoon when you notice it. It may seem strange to you to intentionally let bacteria grow on and near your food, but the strong, sour taste that denotes a good pickle needs fermentation to really develop. As for doneness, the best and only test is to remove one of your vegetables and inspect it. It should taste crisp and fresh, but distinctly soured in that delightful pickle way. It should *not* be slimy, moldy, or foul-smelling; those signs indicate that something has gone very wrong. If you have any questions about the mixture, throw it out. It's better to start over than to eat a bad pickle!

After you decide that your pickles have hit the taste that you're looking for, you can either rinse them and then jar them for a few weeks in a fresh mixture of 3 parts of good quality vinegar (5 percent acidity) with 1 part filtered water, or you can process and can them to preserve them for up to a year. If you choose to can

you choose to ferment in is important—it should be either earthenware or food-safe plastic or glass, and it should be large or deep enough that the vegetables remain under the brine throughout the fermenting period, since any exposure to air can introduce harmful bacteria to your pickles. If you're finding that your vegetables keep floating to the top of the container, you'll need to weigh them down with a heavy plate, or get creative and use a zip-topped bag filled them, you'll need to remove and rinse your pickles, strain and boil the brine they're fermenting in, and then can them using the instructions later in this section.

Quick-Process Pickles

Quick-process (also known as fresh-pack) is a faster and generally easier way to pickle than fermentation. It won't preserve your food nearly as long as the traditional process, but it's tasty and time effective. Instead of bacteria causing fermentation, quick-process pickles rely on vinegar to flavor and preserve the vegetables. Generally, you'll place your produce in a glass jar or food-safe container, and then cover your vegetables with a boiled mixture of vinegar, salt, sugar, and spices. The pickles should then be covered and left at room temperature for approximately 24 hours to allow the flavors to penetrate before being transferred to the refrigerator. Prepared in this way, pickles will last for a few weeks if kept cold. If you'd like to keep your pickles for longer, you'll need to follow the instructions in the canning section for packing and processing your pickles. If quick-process pickles are canned in a sterile manner, they can last for a few months. A quick note, though: if you ever notice your quick-process pickle solution starting to look cloudy, that's a signal to toss the pickles. A cloudy solution is acceptable if you are making fermented pickles, but for nonfermented pickles, it can indicate yeast spoilage. Sometimes, using regular salt instead of pickling or canning salt can also cause cloudiness, as can preparing your pickles in a reactive (any container that is not ceramic, glass, stainless steel, or Teflon) container. Even though cloudiness from salt and from a reactive container is not dangerous, it's usually best to toss cloudy quick-process pickles, in case the off-color is caused by yeast.

Fruit Pickles, Relishes, and Chutneys

Fruit pickles, chutneys, and relishes are all derivatives of the quick-process method of pickling. They are largely unfermented, with the exception of some preserved lemons and limes, and you generally pickle them by covering them in a boiling vinegar-sugar solution. You'll notice as you make them that fruit pickles will take significantly more sugar and less salt than nonfruit pickles, but it's very important not to dilute the vinegar with water—vinegar should always remain at a concentration at or above 5 percent. More sugar can offset the sour tang of the vinegar (unless you enjoy pungent flavors), as can substituting a flavored vinegar like apple cider vinegar or rice wine vinegar. Those options also add a subtle taste that will blend well with Asian flavors. Fruits, relishes, and chutneys should always be canned for storage, unless you are planning to eat them within a few days.

Even though these methods cover most of the pickles that you'll be making, you should treat these overviews primarily as general guidelines. Make sure to check the specific recipe that you're making for any noteworthy changes to the processes outlined here. In general, the longer you plan on storing the pickle, the more chance that you'll need to take some additional steps to ensure safe canning.

STORING and Canning Your CULINARY Crop

Unless you're going to be consuming your pickles within a week or two, you'll most likely be canning them for long-term storage. This preservation method demands a certain attention to detail, but when done properly, it can preserve your pickles for months at a time. Canning used to be thought of as something Granny did, but not anymore. Besides the obvious rewards of preserving and intensifying the flavors of the pickles, many chefs have come to love the hands-on nostalgia of the process itself—you might be one of them!

Tools of the Trade

The most important piece of equipment in your canning adventures is the canner itself, but a lot of people don't know what type of canner to get, or when to use pressure canning versus a hot water bath. The simple rule of thumb is that all high-acid foods go into a hot-water-bath canner. Everything else (low-acid foods, including all nonpickled vegetables, meat, fish, poultry, and dried beans) must be processed in a pressure canner. High-acid foods are all fruit products and anything pickled with vinegar—this includes pickles, relishes, and vinegar-based sauces. All of the pickles that we cover in this book can be successfully canned with the hot water method, so it should be your default method unless a pickle recipe specifically calls for a different tactic. The hot water bath increases the temperature in the canning jar enough to kill bacteria, and it also pushes out air bubbles as the content expands. As the jars cool, the air pressure creates the seal that makes the lid pop—the final product should look like any other well-sealed jar that you would buy at the grocery store or co-op.

Aside from the canner, you'll need several other items if you're going to begin canning your pickles. Now is the time to take an inventory of your canning supplies and equipment and start gathering screwbands, lids,

and jars. Check out your local thrift shops and see if you can get a supply of Mason jars cheap. You may have to ask because they don't always put out jars. Also post a note on your local Freecycle network (*www.freecycle.org*); sometimes you can get canning equipment there, in which case all it costs is the gas to go pick it up. The following list might seem like an unreasonable amount of gear for such a nostalgic practice, but once you have everything you need, you'll find that it will take just minutes to prep your gourmet pickles for storage.

BASIC CANNING EQUIPMENT

* Water-bath canner (you can use a large stockpot with a lid, but any pot used as a water-bath canner must have a rack to keep the jars off the bottom)
* Canning jars—pints, quarts, and jelly Mason jars
* Lids and rings
* Screwbands
* Large spoons for mixing and stirring
* Metal soup ladles
* Sharp paring knives
* Veggie peelers
* Canning funnel
* Colander and/or large strainer
* Large slotted spoons
* Measuring cups and spoons
* Squeezer or juicer
* Food mill, food processor, and/or blender
* Canning-jar lifter and lid wand
* Plastic stirrer for getting air bubbles out of jars
* Kitchen timer
* Cheesecloth for making spice balls
* Pickling or canning salt
* Kitchen towels
* Aprons
* Disposable rubber gloves
* Long-handled jar scrubber
* Kitchen scale (optional)
* Jelly bags (optional)
* Zester, mandolin, melon baller, apple peeler, or cherry pitter (optional)

Only quality Mason jars are safe for canning. As a home chef and DIYer, you probably appreciate thriftiness and enjoy reusing and repurposing, but please, don't try to save money by reusing commercially bought condiment jars, even if they're made of glass. Commercial jars like mayonnaise and peanut butter were designed for one-time use only—they may crack or shatter in the middle of your water bath, leaving you with quite a mess to clean up. And, while the old bail-wire jars look pretty and seem like they come from the era of pickling and canning, they're no longer recommended for the process. Save the antique jars for storage purposes!

Make sure to get canning jars that will fit the amount and size of the pickles you're planning on making. Canning and pickling jars generally are sold in half-pint, pint, and quart sizes with wide and regular mouths. Wide-mouth jars are convenient for packing such foods as whole tomatoes and peach halves. For the most part, though, you'll probably be dicing your produce into small, even shapes so that they really get the full effect of your brine. There's nothing wrong with pickling large items, but remember that it's often the smallest and most intensely flavored morsels that really make a dish a culinary standout.

Canning Preparation

Before you start canning, make sure to read your recipe at least twice and get your ingredients together. Organize the supplies and equipment you'll need to complete your project. There's nothing worse than realizing halfway through your project that you're missing some key piece.

Next, prepare your workspace. You'll need counter space for preparing your foods as well as space for filling your jars once your pickles are prepped. Before you even consider starting to chop, dice, julienne, or otherwise work on your pickles, take a second to figure out exactly how many jars your recipe calls for. Make sure to

examine your jars carefully, checking for cracks or chips. If you have a sterilizing cycle on your dishwasher, put your jars in and run it. Otherwise, use a bottle brush to scrub them inside and out, rinse them in hot water, and sterilize them by boiling them for 10 minutes in a stockpot or water-bath canner. Meanwhile, your lids should be placed in a pan of lightly simmering hot water to kill bacteria and soften the rubber sealing compound. Turn off the simmering water once your lids are in, and let them

shatter. If the jar shatters, you've lost your pickles, but if your countertop shatters, you've lost your paycheck!

Remember to leave the proper amount of headspace in your jar as you fill it—a general rule is about ¼ inch for pickles, preserves, and most other water-bath-processed foods. This is just a generalization, however. Recipes that require a different amount of headspace will specify it in the recipe steps. Just be sure not to overfill your containers, since you don't want fermented liquid seeping out of the jars in your refrigerator!

The last step before processing is removing any air bubbles from the jar. Usually, you can't actually see the air bubbles, but you can take care of any hidden ones by gently stirring the contents of the jar with a plastic stirrer (a wide, plastic knife works great). Make sure you've allowed a moment for the contents to cool slightly before you use any sort of thin plastic that isn't heatproof. Use a damp kitchen towel to wipe the outer rims. Then put on a lid and screw the band firmly. Make sure you don't overtighten your screwbands—an overly tight screwband can buckle in the canner. If that happens, you'll end up with pickles that you can't store safely—not that it's always a bad thing to have to eat your pickles in large quantities immediately!

Processing Pickles

In a typical water bath, sealed jars are placed on a rack and covered with water that rises 1–2 inches above their tops. Put a lid on your water bath, crank up the heat,

remain in the hot water while you treat your jars. This step might seem like a pain, but it's definitely important for safe canning. Run the dishwasher while you're practicing your knife skills with the pickles, or boil your jars while you're firing up a vinegar mixture on the other burner. When it's time to fill the jars, place an old terrycloth bath towel folded in half or two terrycloth kitchen towels on your counter. Never put your jars on an uncovered countertop; it could crack or shatter when you fill a jar with hot food and/or liquid, or the jar itself could crack or and begin timing once the water starts boiling. Most recipes will ask you to process pickles for about 10 minutes to make sure that all of the harmful bacteria has been destroyed. Of course, follow the guidelines in your recipe for the exact times! Once you've hit your mark, remove the jars with a jar lifter. Don't use tongs—you could drop your pickles and either break your jar or splash yourself with boiling water. Then place them on a towel-covered counter to cool for 12–24 hours.

Once the jars are cool enough to touch, take a second to check the seals by pressing your thumb down in the middle of the lid. If the lid seems to give and come back up, the jar isn't sealed. If you're not sure, tap the center of the lid with a knife. It should sound like a bell; a muffled sound means the jar isn't sealed right. What happens if your jar doesn't seal properly? All is not lost! You have several options here. One is to put your pickles in the refrigerator and use them soon. Whip up a salad of pickled vegetables and a nice, strong goat cheese, or melt some paninis with a healthy dose of pickles to cut through the savory flavor. If that's not an option for you, you can try reprocessing the jar within 24 hours of the original effort. If you're going to do this, open the jar, make sure the lid has a clean surface, try changing out the lid, and put everything back in your canner.

After your jars have rested for 12–24 hours, wash them off and move them into the refrigerator, unless the recipe specifically calls for a period of room temperature storage. Fermented pickles will already be soured from their month under brine and can go straight to the refrigerator to slow the fermentation process, but some quick pickles benefit from a few days at room temperature before they are stored—if the recipe does not specify, however, you should refrigerate your canned pickles after processing. Unopened fermented pickles can keep for up to a year under refrigeration after being canned, and most vinegar pickles will last a few months.

It's also important, when you refrigerate your pickles, to write their creation date on the jar. Writing the date might feel foolish to you, but if you're making a lot of pickles, you'll soon start to lose track of what was pickled when. Any restaurant walk-in refrigerator is labeled meticulously, for this same reason. And even with your jars clearly labeled, always check for signs of spoilage. The most obvious sign is the loss of a vacuum seal on the jar and mold growing inside. (Remember, mold is only okay during active fermentation, and even then, it should be on the liquid, not on the pickles.) Other indicators of spoilage include gas bubbles, odd coloring, and foul smells. There is a strong distinction between the acidic tang of a pickle and the terrible odor of spoiled food. Never test suspect food—throw it out!

SAFETY
and Troubleshooting

At sea level, water boils at 212°F. This is the processing temperature for all high-acid and pickled foods. It is the temperature at which molds, yeasts, and some bacteria are destroyed. By processing canned pickles at this temperature, you ensure that unopened, they'll stay fresh in your refrigerator for months at a time. Pay close attention to the canning instructions given in this or any canning guide. Extensive instructions on safe home canning can be obtained from County Extension Services or from the USDA (*www.usda.gov*).

All steps of any pickling or canning project should be carried through as rapidly as possible. Follow the slogan, "Two hours from harvest to container." Work quickly with small amounts of food at a time, since any delay will result in loss of flavor and nutritive value. Additionally, following these simple rules will make your efforts more successful and satisfying:

- **Use prime products; discard any parts with defects.**

- **Keep same-sized items together in jars for even processing.**

- **Wash hands, tools, and ingredients thoroughly. Be fastidious!**

- **Always use a rack on the bottom of your canner to set jars on to avoid breakage and ensure water circulation. Do not use a folded towel; this is not safe.**

- **Follow up-to-date recommendations for detailed procedures in canning, available in USDA or Extension publications. Check for updates regularly.**

Finally, have fun! While the rules sound like drudgery, they're really not difficult. With just a little practice you'll find the preparations and mechanisms come quite naturally—and you'll have a plethora of wonderful pickles to enjoy.

Troubleshooting Pickling Problems

You've followed the instructions, preserved them properly, and still something's gone wrong. What's a cook to do when the pickles turn out less than perfect? This list includes common problems and their solutions.

* Bitter pickles indicate too much vinegar; check the recipe. Note: this can also be caused by using salt substitutes. Any salt or salt substitute other than canning salt has the potential to alter your pickle products, and they should all be avoided, if possible.

* Cloudy pickles are a warning that your pickles may have spoiled if they were fresh-packed. The introduction of an airborne yeast, the use of metal pans, the addition of table salt, and the use of hard water during production can also have this effect. A spoiled fresh-pack pickle will generally seem slimy or smell funny as well. If there are no other signs of spoilage, you can eat the pickles, though to be safe, you might want to discard any cloudy fresh-pack pickles anyway.

* Discolored pickles are usually the fault of the pan or hard water, but strong spices can also bleed over into pickles, giving them a different hue. As long as these pickles smell fine and aren't slimy to the touch, they're generally okay to eat.

* Green- or blue-tinted garlic isn't cause for concern. It just means that the garlic absorbed the metals in your cooking utensils or the garlic you used was young. It's still perfectly safe to eat.

* Hollow cucumbers are safe to eat. The cucumber may have been too big or may have been hollow when canning. If a cucumber floats in water, it's not a good pickling cucumber. The brine may also have been too weak or too strong.

* Pale coloring may mean your produce was exposed to light or was of poor quality. These are okay to eat, although a poor quality cucumber will make a poor quality pickle. If you are fermenting your pickles and they have a light or dull color, they probably need some additional fermentation time before eating.

* Dark coloring in the liquid may result from minerals in the water, the use of different vinegar (like malt vinegar), overcooking, or the use of iodized salt in processing. If you notice new dark coloring in a recipe that you've made before without the color changing, you may have encountered spoilage. When in doubt, throw it out!

* Moldy, scummy brine on any pickles except for fermented pickles is a sign that your food has begun to spoil. Throw these pickles out. If you are making fermented

pickles, the mold is to be expected, and can be removed as often as needed.

❄ Pink pickles may result if you use overly ripe dill in your pickle blend. The introduction of yeast is another possible reason. If the pickles are soft, the liquid cloudy, or the food feels slimy, it's likely a yeast problem and they should be discarded.

Slimy pickles can be the result of a variety of causes. The amount of salt or vinegar used in the mix may not have been sufficient, the pickles may not have been totally covered by brine, the canning process may not have been followed correctly, yeast may have been introduced, moldy spices may have been used, jars may have been improperly sealed, or the pickles may have been kept in an area that was too hot. These are not safe to eat.

Bland pickles may result from the use of cucumbers that were not meant for pickling. Store-bought cucumbers often have a waxy coating. The brine can't penetrate this, so your pickles are less flavorful. If you must use this type of cucumber, slice and salt it for about 1 hour, then rise and pickle. This will open the pores, letting the brine in.

Shriveled pickles may mean the vinegar is too strong, the salt concentration too high, or the pickles over-processed. Measure carefully! These aren't dangerous to eat, but they likely will be unpleasantly acidic. It's best to throw them out.

Mixed flavors usually mean the size of the vegetables wasn't even. The larger the cut, the more time a vegetable takes to accept flavor.

Mushy pickles can result from using the wrong type of cucumber or over-processing. If you have a choice of what to buy or grow, look for Lemon, Little Leaf, Saladin, and Edmonson cucumbers. You can use food-grade alum or grape leaves in the bottom of the jar to improve crispness.

Mold or dirt on a jar (unless you're actively fermenting) often indicates it wasn't properly sealed; some of the brine has gotten out onto the rim, meaning that bacteria can also get into the jar. Don't eat these. Whenever you're confronted with a jar you don't feel quite right about, it's usually best to err on the side of caution and throw it out.

COOKING with Your Creations

Once you begin using the recipes in this book to make pickled fruits, vegetables, and meats, you'll want to expand your culinary repertoire by incorporating your preserves into finished dishes! Parts III and IV of this book contain numerous recipes for appetizers, entrées, sides, and even drinks that use pickled ingredients in either a starring or supporting role. But you may soon find that you want to move past the recipes listed here, and it's important to have some general guidelines if you're planning to use pickles full-time in your cooking.

First, it's important to know that unlike the recipes for the pickles themselves, cooking with pickles is far more open to improvisation and interpretation. As long as you're starting with safe pickles, you can treat them anyway that you want and still get good outcomes. Of course, you'll need to make sure foods are fully cooked as you always would, but there's no need to be measuring out vinegar or salt solutions at this point!

The key to getting the maximum mileage out of your pickles is knowing how to balance them with other contrasting flavors. Think about the flavors that your pickle gives you. Take a bite, and try to notice all of the distinct sensations and tastes that your mouth and tongue can detect. Is your pickle just salty and tangy? Does it have a hint (or more than a hint) of sweetness? Is it spicy? Noticing the subtle variations in flavor will help you do a better job pairing your preserves with proper recipes. Here are some basic flavor guidelines that can be used as a jumping-off point for creating some recipe combinations. Of course, your tastes are unique, so you should always follow your tongue to what it likes best!

For salty/tangy pickles: Think classics, like sandwiches, paninis, burgers, and so forth. The more savory, fatty, and heavy the food is, the more help it will get from a tangy pickle. Red meat in particular has an affinity for

Pan-Seared Duck Breast with Shallots, see Part III

pickles—burgers are the obvious example here, but a nice rich pastrami or corned beef sandwich with melted cheese and pickles is heaven on a plate. Salty and tangy pickles are also fantastic when eaten by themselves, and pickled Mediterranean vegetables are great with Italian food. Think of a grilled Mediterranean chicken breast with pickled peppers and capers acting as counterpoints.

For spicy pickles: Spicy pickles are a fun complement to cooling dishes, like cold Asian peanut noodles or American pasta salad. Of course, any dish that would benefit from hot sauce or peppers is also a candidate for the more upscale and complex spicy pickle. Californian fish tacos, Vietnamese Banh Mi (see Part III), and even Tex-Mex barbecue skillets all do well with a dose of pickled heat.

For fruit pickles or sweet pickles: Fruit pickles can be said to have the most complex taste of any pickle—a balance of sweetness and sourness that tastes completely gourmet. Pickled fruits are great complements to savory roasted meats, especially during the holidays—think of a rich and decadent rib roast with pickled plums to brighten and sweeten the dish. Fruits are also excellent as an accent topping to a dessert, especially if you want to be unexpected and playful. Rich ice cream with shortcake and lightly pickled figs is a grown-up version of the Fig Newtons you may have enjoyed as a child!

Pickled fruits are also wonderful in salads and antipastos, served with prosciutto and complex cheeses.

Of course, these are just a few of the many ways you can utilize the gourmet pickles that you'll soon be making. The recipes in the following sections will give you more than 100 pickles and recipes that you can then use again and again in various combinations as your taste buds dictate. Once you have your pickles, don't be afraid to experiment with tastes, textures, and contrasts in your dishes. Pickles are the ultimate improvisational counterpoint, and there are no hard-and-fast rules to where they can and can't be used. You're only limited by your imagination!

PART II
RECIPES FOR PICKLES

The first step to building the gourmet dishes in this book is to have a wide variety of pickles that you can draw upon to complement the other ingredients in your recipe. You got an overview of pickling mechanics and the basic steps of the process in Part I, and here in Part II you'll find the recipes for making more than 50 different kinds of pickles, including vegetables, fruits, relishes, spicy pickles, and even preserved and pickled meats and seafood. Any of these recipes can be enjoyed as-is on their own, or you can use them as a sensational enhancement to any prepared dishes you'll be cooking. For now, though, gather your jars, hit the farmers' market or the garden, and clear your counters, because it's time to get pickling!

DILL PICKLES

These pickles have a mild, tasty flavor that echoes the subtle sweetness of the apple cider vinegar. You could substitute a wide variety of vegetables for the pickles.

YIELDS 1 GALLON

6 tablespoons pickling or canning salt

½ gallon water

1 cup apple cider vinegar, plus more to fill

4 pounds small pickling cucumbers

1 cup fresh dill leaf

2 tablespoons black peppercorns

½ cup packaged pickling spice blend

1. Make the brine by dissolving the salt in the water. Stir in the apple cider vinegar.
2. Mix the whole cucumbers with the dill, peppercorns, and pickling spice blend. Place mixture into a glass 1 gallon jar.
3. Pour the brine over the cucumbers. Add more apple cider vinegar and fill to the top of the jar. It may take up to an extra ½ cup of vinegar. Make sure all cucumbers are covered in brine. Cover the jar tightly with a lid.
4. Place the jar of cucumbers in the refrigerator and let sit. They will be ready to eat after 2 days. They become more sour after 1–2 weeks. Since these pickles are not processed or canned, you should consume them within 10–14 days, for safety.

Worldwide Pickles

In Europe, vegetables commonly pickled include peppers, tomatoes, olives, eggplant, carrots, cauliflower, beets, and mushrooms. In Asia, nontraditional pickles include mangoes, papaya, pineapple, and ume plum, as well as garlic, ginger, and shallots.

FREEZER CUCUMBERS

Instead of preserving these pickles through canning, you preserve them through freezing. Frozen pickles will keep for at least 6-8 months in the freezer. Once you're ready to eat them, thaw them out, and they'll last for about a week.

YIELDS 2 QUARTS

12 cups thinly sliced cucumbers

4 cups thinly sliced sweet onions

3 cups sugar

3 cups white vinegar

1 teaspoon pickling or canning salt

1 teaspoon mustard seeds

1 teaspoon celery seeds

1. Place cucumbers and onions in a large nonreactive bowl.
2. Mix remaining ingredients in a saucepan; bring to a boil. Stir to dissolve sugar.
3. Pour over cucumbers. Put a plate on top of cucumbers so they stay below brine; let sit at room temperature 24 hours.
4. Move into freezer-safe containers, leaving a small amount of space for expansion in the freezer. If you'd prefer to turn this recipe into a traditional canned recipe, this blend can be successfully canned using a hot-water-bath method for 15 minutes. In a freezer, the cucumbers will keep for several months, and if canned, the pickles will keep for up to a year, in a cold place.

HEIRLOOM MUSTARD
PICKLES

These are the kinds of pickles often seen on our grandparents' tables. While the spices may change a little, the passion these pickles inspire remains consistent.

YIELDS 4 QUARTS

4 cups onions

4 cups cucumbers

4 cups small green tomatoes

1 medium cauliflower

2 sweet peppers

1 gallon water

2 cups pickling or canning salt

Pinch alum (optional)

4 cups sugar

3 tablespoons celery seed

⅔ cup mustard

4¼ cups white vinegar

1. Cut vegetables into 1-inch pieces. Put in a large bowl; cover with water, salt, and alum.

2. Put a plate over top of vegetables so they stay below brine; leave at room temperature 24 hours.

3. The next day, warm entire mixture to boiling; remove from heat and drain vegetables. Immediately put into sterilized jars (if canning) or freezer-safe containers (if freezing).

4. Put remaining ingredients in a large pot; simmer until thickened. Pour sauce evenly over pickles. Make sure to get all the air bubbles out if canning. Leave ¼-inch headspace in the jars; process 10 minutes in a hot water bath. If freezing, remember to leave extra space for freezer expansion.

5. Canned pickles have a shelf life of about 1 year, if stored in a refrigerator or a cool place. Frozen pickles last 6–8 months.

PUNGENT PICKLED GARLIC

This recipe makes a nice snack or may be used in garnishing various beverages. Pickled garlic is also a wonderful complement to any pungent Chinese, Thai, or Malaysian dish.

YIELDS 2 PINTS

2 cups white vinegar

½ cup red wine vinegar

1 cup dry white wine

1 tablespoon pickling or canning salt

1 tablespoon sugar

1 tablespoon oregano or basil (optional)

12 large garlic cloves, peeled

1. Bring vinegars, wine, salt, sugar, and spices to a boil in a small saucepot for 1 minute. Let cool momentarily.
2. Separate garlic evenly between prepared canning jars.
3. Pour hot brine over garlic, leaving ½-inch head space. Cap the jars.
4. Process in hot water bath 10 minutes. Cool, label and store. The garlic will keep in a cold place for up to a year.

SWEET RED ONIONS

Red onions have a vibrant color and flavor that melds nicely with Latin cuisine. The pickling process removes much of the harsh smell from the onions, leaving you with a mildly sweet and sour vegetable with a tasty undercurrent of onion goodness!

YIELDS 1 PINT

⅔ **cup white vinegar**

Juice of 1 lime

2 tablespoons pickling or canning salt

1 tablespoon sugar

1 teaspoon red chili flakes (optional)

1 red onion, peeled and sliced into rings or thin strips

1. In a medium saucepan, heat all of the ingredients except the onion over medium-low heat until the salt and sugar have fully dissolved. Turn up the heat slightly and bring the mixture to a quick boil.

2. Add the onion and stir to combine, making sure that all parts of the onion are submerged. Lower the heat and simmer for 45 seconds.

3. Let the mixture cool on the stovetop until lukewarm.

4. Transfer the mixture to a glass jar or other storage container; cover and refrigerate. Pickled red onions generally taste best when served cool. These unprocessed pickles will keep for a week or two, refrigerated.

BRINED CAPERS

If you buy salted capers, rinse them before you pickle them or they'll be way too salty. In pickled form, capers are a nice addition to many Mediterranean dishes.

YIELDS 1 QUART

3 cups capers

4 cups white vinegar

2 teaspoons pickling or canning salt

1 medium red or Spanish onion, thinly sliced

½ lemon, thinly sliced

1 teaspoon pickling spice

2 cloves garlic, peeled and minced

5 peppercorns

½ teaspoon celery seed

½ teaspoon mustard seeds (optional)

1. Combine all ingredients in a pan; bring to a boil for 5 minutes.
2. Pour into a quart container; cap and process 15 minutes in a hot water bath.
3. Cool, label, and store.

Caper Capers

Capers come from a shrub native to the Mediterranean. They are actually a fruit. Capers are seen predominantly in Italian cuisine, where they are often combined with cream cheese, smoked salmon, and certain salsa blends. In ancient times, the Greeks used capers to treat rheumatism.

PICKLED RAMPS

Pickled ramps are a true gourmand's delight. These pungent vegetables work wonders in a garlicky, spicy pasta dish, or dropped into a dirty martini. Pickle as many ramps as you can—their growing season is tragically short.

YIELDS APPROXIMATELY 2–3 PINTS

3 bunches ramps, trimmed and washed

½ cup white vinegar

½ cup white wine vinegar

¾ cup sugar

1 cup water

1 tablespoon pickling or canning salt

1 tablespoon mustard seeds

1 tablespoon black peppercorns

1. Clean the ramps by cutting off their green tops and washing the white stems well under cold running water. You can keep the green tops for another use, but they do not hold up well to pickling.
2. Bring a large pot of water to a boil over high heat on the stovetop. Have a large bowl filled with ice water ready nearby.
3. Drop the ramps into the boiling water, blanching them in boiling water for 30–45 seconds. Remove them to the ice water to stop the cooking process.
4. After the ramps have cooled, drain them, and place them into two or three pint-sized jars.
5. In a small saucepan, bring the vinegars, sugar, water, and salt to a boil. Make sure that the sugar and salt dissolve fully. Once the mixture is boiling, add the mustard seeds and the peppercorns. Pour over the ramps in the jars, and allow to cool before covering them and moving to the refrigerator. The ramps will keep for a few weeks.

DILLY BEANS

Dilly beans take green beans, which tend to be bland, and inject them with a major dose of taste. Sour, salty, spicy, and delicious, these are some of the best pickles for out-of-the-jar snacking.

YIELDS APPROXIMATELY 2 PINTS

1 pound green beans

2 cloves garlic, peeled

1 tablespoon red pepper flakes

3 teaspoons dill seed

1 cup white vinegar

½ cup white wine vinegar

½ cup water

3 tablespoons pickling or canning salt

1. Wash the green beans and trim their ends so that they are uniform. If needed, cut them further so that they will fit easily inside of the jars you are using to can them.
2. Divide the beans into sterilized canning jars, along with the garlic, pepper flakes, and dill seed.
3. In a small saucepan, bring the vinegars, water, and pickling salt to a boil, until the salt dissolves.
4. Pour the pickling mixture over the green beans and cap the jars.
5. Process the jars in a boiling water bath for 10 minutes before refrigerating.

HOT OKRA

Pickled okra is a quintessential Southern delicacy, eaten by itself or enjoyed on a relish tray or with a heaping plate of barbecue. You can adjust the heat in these pickles as you like!

YIELDS APPROXIMATELY 2 PINTS

1 pound okra pods

3 cloves garlic, peeled

1 tablespoon fresh chopped dill

1 tablespoon red pepper flakes

½ cup white vinegar

½ cup white wine vinegar

4 tablespoons pickling or canning salt

1½ cups water

1. Wash and trim the okra pods so they all have a short, manageable shape.
2. Divide the okra pods, garlic, dill, and pepper flakes evenly into two sterilized pint-sized jars.
3. In a small saucepan over medium-high heat, bring the two varieties of vinegar, the pickling salt, and the water to a hard boil.
4. Carefully pour the boiling liquid over the vegetables in the two jars.
5. Seal the jars, and process them in a hot water bath for 10 minutes. Keep the okra in a cold place for up to a year.

PICKLED CARROTS

Pickled vegetables are very popular in Cantonese cuisine; look for them on the menu the next time you dine at a Cantonese restaurant.

YIELDS 1½ CUPS

1½ cups (12 ounces) baby carrots

⅓ cup rice vinegar

⅓ cup sugar

¼ teaspoon pickling or canning salt

1 tablespoon allspice berries

2 cups water

1. Wash the baby carrots. Place them in a nonreactive bowl or jar that's large enough to hold them comfortably.
2. In a medium saucepan, bring the remaining ingredients to a boil, stirring to dissolve the sugar.
3. Pour the liquid over the carrots, cover the container, and refrigerate for at least 2 days. The carrots will last for about a week in the refrigerator.

PICKLED ASPARAGUS

This is a type of refrigerator pickling but this recipe is also safe for hot-water-bath canning. If you choose to do hot-water-bath canning, follow proper safety procedures and process for 10 minutes.

YIELDS 3 PINTS

3½ pounds asparagus, cut into 6-inch pieces

3 cloves garlic, peeled

1 shallot, minced

3 bay leaves

1½ teaspoons black peppercorns

1½ teaspoons dill seeds

1 tablespoon fresh dill

1½ teaspoons yellow mustard seed

2 cups water

2 cups white vinegar

¼ cup pickling salt

1. Evenly divide the asparagus, garlic, shallot, bay leaves, peppercorns, dill seeds, dill, and mustard seeds among 3 wide-mouth pint jars.

2. In a saucepan, bring the water, vinegar, and salt to a boil, stirring to dissolve the salt. Ladle over the asparagus. Close the jars. Allow them to come to room temperature and then refrigerate.

3. Wait 1 week before eating. Keep refrigerated at all times.

Canning

Canning fruits and vegetables is a great way to preserve food at its peak. Pickling is an easy place to start. Even unprocessed pickles keep for weeks or even months in the refrigerator.

PICKLED MUSHROOMS

These pickles are great to serve with a Mediterranean-themed meal. A variation is to add green or kalamata olives. This dish will only keep refrigerated for up to 3 days, because of the low acidity in the pickling mixture.

YIELDS APPROXIMATELY 1 PINT

1 pound white button mushrooms or other variety

¼ cup olive oil

¼ cup rice vinegar

½ teaspoon pickling or canning salt

**1 teaspoon fresh dill, minced,
   or ½ teaspoon dried dill**

2 tablespoons parsley, minced

1 clove garlic, peeled and minced

Zest of 1 lemon

1. Slice mushrooms thinly. Place mushrooms in a pint-sized glass jar.
2. Mix olive oil, rice vinegar, salt, dill, parsley, garlic, and lemon zest together.
3. Pour herb mixture over mushrooms and cover.
4. Refrigerate overnight and serve. The mushrooms will keep for about three days in the refrigerator.

SWEET AND SOUR BEETS

These flavorful pickles can jazz up a plate with bright red color. Serve pickled beets with fresh green salad.

YIELDS APPROXIMATELY 2 CUPS

2 medium beets

Water, as needed

½ cup rice vinegar

⅛ teaspoon pickling or canning salt

½ cup apple cider

1 medium bay leaf

1. Slice beets into ¼-inch slices.
2. In a small saucepan, cover beets with water. Bring to boil, lower heat, and simmer for 15 minutes. Drain. Place beets in a pint-sized glass jar.
3. Bring rice vinegar, salt, apple cider, and bay leaf to a boil, lower heat, and simmer for 2 minutes.
4. Pour vinegar mixture over beets and cover. Refrigerate at least overnight.
5. Drain before serving. The beets will keep for a few days to a week in the refrigerator.

NASTURTIUM

The flavor of the nasturtium is very similar to capers and far less expensive. Note, however, that it's essential to use the green pods because mature pods are unsuitable for consumption.

YIELDS 1 CUP

2 tablespoons pickling or canning salt

1 cup water

½ cup green nasturtium seed pods

⅔ cup white wine vinegar

¼ cup red wine vinegar

2 teaspoons sugar

1 bay leaf

Pinch dried thyme

1. Mix salt and water together with nasturtiums. Soak 3 days, making sure the pods stay beneath water's surface.

2. Strain; put in a pint-sized canning jar.

3. Mix vinegars with remaining ingredients; bring to a boil.

4. Pour over pods. Cap and seal in a hot water bath 10 minutes. These processed pickles will keep for up to a year in a cold place.

Nasturtium's Story

This flower originated in Peru. Today, there are well over thirty varieties of nasturtiums in the world. The petals have been used for hundreds of years in salads, and they're high in vitamin C. If you love birds, grow nasturtiums to attract hummingbirds.

SHALLOT CONFITURE

This is delightful to use as a condiment served either warm or cold with meats, or apply as a marinade. Shallot Confiture is a labor-intensive process that involves some rudimentary canning procedures, but the end results are well worth it!

YIELDS 7 PINTS

3 pounds shallots, peeled, root ends intact

1½ cups pickling or canning salt

8 cups apple cider vinegar

4½ cups granulated sugar

4 cardamom pods, crushed

2 teaspoons dried lemon zest

2 cinnamon sticks

4–6 small dried red chili peppers

2½ teaspoons whole cloves

1 tablespoon whole black peppercorns

1. *Day one.* Peel the shallots, leaving the root ends intact. Place them in a nonmetallic bowl; sprinkle with canning salt. Add enough water to cover, stirring carefully to dissolve the salt. Put a plate on top of the shallots to submerge them completely. Cover with a clean cotton dish towel; put in a cool place and let sit for 24 hours.

2. *Day two.* Drain and rinse the shallots thoroughly in cool water; dry on paper towels. Pour the vinegar and sugar into a stockpot; stir well. Make a spice ball using a doubled square of cheesecloth and all the spices. Add the spice ball to the stockpot. Heat on medium heat until sugar has completely dissolved. Raise the heat and bring to a boil; boil for 10 minutes. Add the shallots; simmer gently for 15 minutes. Remove stockpot from heat; cover, and let sit for 24 hours.

3. *Day three.* Return shallots to stove and slowly bring them to a boil; turn down heat and simmer for 15 minutes. Remove stockpot from heat; cover, and let sit for 24 hours.

4. *Day four.* Return shallots to stove and slowly bring them to a boil once more. Simmer gently until the shallots are golden brown and translucent. Discard spice ball. Ladle into sterilized jars. Use a plastic knife or plastic straw to remove air pockets. Cap and seal. Process in a water-bath canner for 10 minutes. Store in a cool, dark, dry place for 2–3 months to allow flavors to meld, and consume within a year or so.

GREEN TOMATO PICCALILLI

This can be served as a side dish or as a brightly colored condiment, especially for hamburgers and hot dogs.

YIELDS 6–8 PINTS

16 cups green tomatoes, finely chopped
½ head green cabbage, finely chopped
½ cup pickling or canning salt
Water, for soaking vegetables
4 cups apple cider vinegar
1½ cups dark brown sugar
½ tablespoon mustard seeds
½ tablespoon ground cinnamon
1 tablespoon black pepper
⅛ teaspoon crushed red pepper flakes
½ tablespoon ground allspice
1 tablespoon ground ginger
1 tablespoon dill seed

1. *Day one.* Combine vegetables and salt; cover with water and soak overnight.
2. *Day two.* Drain and rinse vegetables.
3. In a large pot, combine remaining ingredients; bring to a boil.
4. Add drained vegetables; return mixture to a boil.
5. Reduce heat; simmer until vegetables are tender, about 30 minutes.
6. Pack hot mixture into sterilized pint jars. Cover; process in boiling bath for 15 minutes. This processed mixture will keep for up to a year in a cold place.

Piccalilli

Traditional piccalilli is a mixture of chopped vegetables with piquant spices such as mustard. Common components include cabbage, tomato, cauliflower, carrot, and onion, but nearly anything can go into the pickling mixture.

SWEET MINTED EGGPLANT

These pickles do not need to be chilled for serving. In fact, they're tastiest at room temperature.

YIELDS APPROXIMATELY 3 CUPS

1 pound small eggplants, cut into ½-inch-thick rounds

1 tablespoon pickling or canning salt

2 tablespoons lemon juice

2 tablespoons white vinegar

2 tablespoons honey

½ cup extra-virgin olive oil

2 tablespoons minced garlic

⅓ cup chopped fresh mint

Grated zest of 1 lemon

¼ teaspoon dried red pepper flakes

Salt to taste

Pepper to taste

1. Arrange the eggplant slices on a baking sheet, and sprinkle them with the pickling salt; let stand 30 minutes.
2. Preheat oven broiler.
3. In a small bowl, mix lemon juice, vinegar, honey, olive oil, herbs, and spices together; toss eggplant pieces to coat evenly.
4. Remove eggplant; save the honey-vinegar blend for later.
5. Under the broiler, grill eggplant lightly, about 3 minutes on each side.
6. Toss the eggplant back into honey-vinegar blend; pack into a small jar. Since these are unprocessed pickles, they should be stored in the refrigerator, and should be used within a week.

SPICED ARTICHOKE HEARTS

Serve these as appetizers or as a topping to either green salad or pasta salad to shake things up a bit. The flavor improves if served with a little olive oil.

YIELDS 2 PINTS

2½ cups fresh or frozen artichoke hearts, defrosted

½ cup white wine vinegar

¼ cup red wine vinegar

½ cup water

4 whole cloves garlic, peeled

¼ teaspoon thyme

¼ teaspoon parsley

¼ teaspoon rosemary

½ teaspoon basil

½ teaspoon oregano

⅛ teaspoon dried red pepper flakes

1. In a medium saucepan, blanch the artichoke hearts in boiling water for 30 seconds, then chill them by running them under cold water. Drain them in a colander.
2. Place hearts in equal quantities in four ½-pint jars.
3. Mix together remaining ingredients; heat in a saucepan to boiling.
4. Pour over hearts, leaving ½-inch headspace; cap and seal.
5. Process 15 minutes in hot-water canner. Let cool; then check lids. These processed artichokes will stay good for up to a year in a cold place.

Artichoke Flower

The artichoke is a kissing cousin to the sunflower, and it probably originated somewhere in the Mediterranean. The part we eat is really a flower bud that could blossom into a 7-inch array if not harvested for food. Currently, there are more than 40 commercial varieties cultivated worldwide.

SAUER**KRAUT**

This recipe is based on a traditional method of making kraut in a brine crock. You'll need a large, earthenware 3-gallon crock.

YIELDS 4 QUARTS

12 pounds cabbage

¼ pound pickling or canning salt

½ tablespoon allspice berries

1. Wash the cabbage head; remove any leaves that have dark spots.
2. Cut cabbage into quarters; remove core and shred into ¼-inch pieces.
3. Mix cabbage with salt; pack firmly into brine crock. With a clean utensil, mash the mixture to draw water out of the cabbage and form a brine.
4. Fill crock, leaving 5 inches of headspace. If the brine that has formed has not covered the cabbage, boil some water, cool it, and then add it to the crock until the cabbage is completely covered.
5. Use a small bowl, plate, or other weight at the top to push the cabbage down; cover crock with an airtight lid.
6. Leave cabbage 5 weeks to ferment (75°F is the best temperature).
7. Move sauerkraut to a nonreactive saucepan; add the allspice and simmer until heated through.
8. Pack hot into jars, leaving ½-inch headspace. Process 20 minutes in hot-water bath for quarts. Sauerkraut should last for up to a year in a cold place.

VEGETABLE MEDLEY

This is a delicious snack when eaten alone, and it is a good addition to salads and burrito wraps.

YIELDS 1 PINT

4 tablespoons packaged pickling spice blend

4 tablespoons pickling or canning salt

1 cup carrot, chopped

½ cup beets, chopped

1 cup daikon radish, chopped

1 cup celery root, chopped

3 cloves garlic, peeled and sliced

2 cups apple cider vinegar

1. Place the pickling spices and salt at the bottom of a 1-gallon glass jar.
2. Place the vegetables and garlic into the jar.
3. Pour in the apple cider vinegar, and then add water and fill to the top of the jar.
4. Place a lid on the jar and shake it to mix up the spices and salt.
5. Gently shake the jar every day. The pickled vegetables will be ready to eat in 2–5 days. They'll keep for a few weeks under refrigeration.

Herbs and Spices for Pickles

Vegetables may be pickled with various herbs and spices, depending on your preference. You might try some of these herbs: juniper berries, dill, mint, marjoram, basil, and orange and lemon zest. For spices, you can experiment with cinnamon sticks, cloves, allspice, pepper, caraway seeds, ginger, mustard seeds, and nutmeg.

PICKLED VEGETABLES AND ARAME

Black strands of arame, a kelp used in Japanese cooking, add extra dimension to this colorful and dynamic pickle. Make different versions of this colorful recipe using various seasonal vegetables. Purple dulse flakes, which support heart function, can be substituted for arame.

YIELDS APPROXIMATELY 3 CUPS

½ **cup celery**

½ **cup carrot**

½ **cup red cabbage**

½ **cup yellow onion**

¼ **cup arame, soaked in water for 30 minutes**

1 **medium bay leaf**

½ **teaspoon olive oil**

½ **cup rice vinegar**

½ **teaspoon pickling or canning salt**

1. Cut vegetables into thin slices. Place sliced vegetables, arame, and bay leaf in a glass jar or a nonreactive bowl.
2. In a separate container, mix the olive oil, rice vinegar, and salt together.
3. Pour marinade over vegetables and cover.
4. Refrigerate overnight and serve. These pickles should be eaten within a few days to maximize freshness.

CORN RELISH

This is a bright, beautiful dish, both visually and flavor-wise. Try it served with crab cakes.

YIELDS 5–6 PINTS

10 cups uncooked sweet baby corn kernels, fresh or thawed from frozen

1 cup sweet red pepper, diced

1 cup sweet green pepper, diced

1 cup celery, diced

½ cup red onion, sliced

½ cup Vidalia onion, diced

1½ cups sugar

2½ cups white vinegar

2 cups water

1 teaspoon pickling or canning salt

2 teaspoons celery seed

2 teaspoons mustard seeds

1. Place all ingredients in a large pan over medium heat. Bring to a fast boil; lower heat and simmer 15 minutes.

2. Hot pack into pint jars, leaving ½-inch headspace. Cap and seal; process in boiling water 15 minutes. Check lids after cool for proper sealing to prevent leakage. As with most canned pickles, Corn Relish will keep for up to a year, stored in a cold place.

CARAMELIZED
RED ONION RELISH

Red onions lend themselves particularly well to becoming a relish. They have high sugar content, caramelize easily, and can get quite sweet when cooked down over a long period of time.

YIELDS 6 PINTS

6 large red onions, peeled and sliced very thinly

¾ cup brown sugar, firmly packed

1 tablespoon extra virgin olive oil

3 cups dry red wine

½ cup balsamic vinegar

½ teaspoon pickling or canning salt

½ teaspoon freshly ground black pepper

1. In a heavy nonstick skillet, combine onions and sugar with olive oil; heat over medium-high heat.
2. Cook uncovered for 25 minutes, or until onions turn golden and start to caramelize, stirring frequently.
3. Stir in wine, vinegar, salt, and pepper; bring to a boil over high heat. Reduce heat to low; cook 15 minutes, or until most of the liquid has evaporated, stirring frequently.
4. Ladle into sterilized jars, leaving ½-inch headspace. Remove air bubbles.
5. Wipe rims. Cap and seal. Process in a water-bath canner for 10 minutes. Check the lids for a solid seal. This relish will keep for up to a year under refrigeration.

GREEN CORIANDER CHUTNEY

This bright green chutney gets an extra pop from the addition of grated coconut. It's particularly good on seafood, but very nice simply spread on toast.

YIELDS APPROXIMATELY 1 CUP

1 bunch coriander (cilantro), stems included

3–4 sprigs of fresh mint

2 serrano chilies, seeded and roughly chopped

3 garlic cloves, peeled and roughly chopped

¼ cup unsweetened grated coconut

1 (1-inch) piece of fresh ginger, peeled and chopped

Juice of 2 fresh lemons

½ teaspoon pickling or canning salt

1. Place all the ingredients in a blender or food processor and blend until smooth.
2. Pour chutney into a jar. It may seem a little thin, but it will thicken into a paste.
3. Store in the refrigerator where it will keep for up to 1 month.

Chutney

Chutneys are condiments and spreads made from cooking down fruit that is flavored with spices. The word comes from the Hindi *catni*, and chutney originated as a South Asian food, though now it is used and made around the world. Chutneys can be made from almost any fruit or vegetable, but common ones found are mango, tomato, and tamarind.

SASSY SUMMER CHUTNEY

This is a sweet-savory blend that can be used as a condiment, side dish, or sauce. If you'd like to can it, use the hot-water-bath method for 15 minutes. If canned, it will keep for up to a year in a cold place.

YIELDS 4 PINTS

1 pound fresh apricots

1 pound fresh peaches

1 pound fresh nectarines

1 pound fresh pears

2 small seedless oranges

20 cloves garlic, peeled and minced

2 tablespoons freshly ground ginger

1 cup golden raisins

1 cup dried cranberries

1 cup apple cider vinegar

1 cup light brown sugar, firmly packed

3 cups sweet onions, finely diced

2 cups orange juice

½ teaspoon ground cinnamon

½ teaspoon ground clove

1 teaspoon pickling or canning salt

½ teaspoon freshly ground allspice

1. Peel and chop the apricots, peaches, nectarines, and pears; put into a large pot. Carefully remove the peel from the oranges and add the peels to the pot.

2. Chop oranges and garlic; add to the pot. Add all remaining ingredients. Bring to a boil, stirring constantly.

3. Reduce heat to low; simmer for 45 minutes, continuing to stir regularly. The chutney will begin to thicken.

4. Cool and move into freezer-safe containers, leaving ¼-inch headspace for expansion. Place in the freezer for up to 6–8 months. Once the chutney is defrosted, use within a week.

MANGO CHUTNEY

Sweet, sour, and spicy all at once, this chutney is great spread onto crackers, or served with fish or chicken.

YIELDS APPROXIMATELY 2 CUPS

3 ripe yellow mangoes, peeled, pitted, and cut into ½-inch cubes

1 (2-inch) piece fresh ginger, peeled and finely minced

2 garlic cloves, peeled and finely minced

½ teaspoon pickling or canning salt

½ teaspoon cayenne pepper

1 cup white vinegar

¾ cup light brown sugar

1. Combine all the ingredients together in a heavy-bottomed saucepan and let simmer over very low heat for 20–30 minutes, until it is very thick.
2. Remove chutney from heat and let cool.
3. When chutney is cooled, transfer to a glass jar and store, covered, in the refrigerator for up to a month.

BLUEBERRY CHUTNEY

Try this sweet chutney on goose, turkey, chicken, and other fowl.

YIELDS 4 PINTS

8 cups fresh blueberries, rinsed and stemmed

2 medium onions, finely chopped

3 cups red wine vinegar

1 cup golden yellow raisins

1 cup dark brown sugar, firmly packed

1 tablespoon mustard seeds

2 tablespoons freshly grated ginger

1 teaspoon ground cinnamon

1 pinch pickling or canning salt

¼ teaspoon ground nutmeg

½ teaspoon dried red pepper flakes

1. Place blueberries in a large stockpot with onion, vinegar, raisins, brown sugar, mustard seeds, ginger, cinnamon, salt, nutmeg, and red pepper flakes. Bring mixture to a boil.
2. Lower heat; simmer, stirring occasionally, about 45 minutes, or until chutney is thick.
3. Ladle hot chutney into sterilized jars, leaving ½-inch headspace. Wipe rims; cap and seal.
4. Process in water-bath canner 15 minutes. Cool.
5. Store in a cold place, either the refrigerator or a cellar, and let the flavors mingle for at least 6–8 weeks before using. This recipe will keep for up to a year unopened.

Blue Food

Blueberries carry the folk names of hurtleberries and bilberries. Unlike so many other fruits, this is one that has its roots in North America. Do not purchase under-ripe blueberries; they don't continue to ripen after harvesting, and you want the sweetest blueberries possible for pickling.

VINEGAR-PACKED PEPPERS

Pickling jalapeños brings out a range of other sour flavors in addition to the heat of the pepper. These are delicious enough to eat as-is, but consider adding them to a Southwestern dish for a piquant kick.

YIELDS 20–25 PEPPERS

1 pound fresh jalapeño peppers, washed

2½ cups water

2½ cups white vinegar

3 tablespoons pickling or canning salt

1 tablespoon sugar

4 garlic cloves, peeled and thinly sliced

2 tablespoons coriander seeds

2 tablespoons black peppercorns

2 bay leaves

1. With a small paring knife, poke each pepper 2 or 3 times, creating small slits for the brine to seep in. Put peppers in a large, clean glass preserving jar or several smaller ones.

2. In a nonreactive saucepan, combine all remaining ingredients and bring to a boil. Reduce heat and let simmer for 2 minutes.

3. Remove brine from heat and pour over peppers. Screw the lids onto the jars and let cool.

4. When peppers are cool, put jars in the refrigerator and let sit for several days. You can eat them after just a few days, but they will taste better if you let them sit for at least a week. The peppers will keep for up to a month.

SALT-CURED THAI CHILIES

This simple recipe works best with fresh red chilies because the salt preserves their bright color and makes them especially striking. Feel free to use whatever kind of chilies you like, and consider adding other vegetables to the mix.

YIELDS 40–50 THAI CHILIES

1 pound fresh red Thai chilies

⅓ cup kosher salt

1. Make sure your chilies are thoroughly dried. Cut off the stems and tips and roughly chop them, keeping the seeds. It's a good idea to wear gloves for this task to avoid chili burns, as you'll be handling quite a few chilies.

2. Place the chopped chilies in a large bowl. Add the salt and mix thoroughly.

3. Place chilies in a large, clean glass jar or several smaller ones. Feel free to pack them to the top, as they will shrink in size. Fill in any excess space at the top with more salt.

4. Screw lids on tightly and leave in a cool place for 2 weeks before using. Once opened, store chilies in the refrigerator for a month.

SPICY DILLS

A hotter take on the classic American dill pickle. Feel free to turn up the heat as you like. These spicy pickles go great with craft beer and a well-marbled hamburger, as long as your guests like heat!

YIELDS 48 PICKLES

12 pickling cucumbers, cut lengthwise into quarters

2 serrano peppers, thinly sliced

2 cups white vinegar

1½ cups water

1 tablespoon coriander seeds

1 tablespoon black peppercorns

1 teaspoon fennel seeds

1 teaspoon crushed red chill pepper flakes

1 bunch dill, roughly chopped

1. Combine all ingredients except dill in a large bowl. Stir and let sit at room temperature for at least 2 hours.
2. Divide dill evenly into 2 or 3 jars. Divide cucumber spears evenly into jars as well.
3. Pour pickling liquid over cucumber spears.
4. Screw lids on and store in the refrigerator for 2 days before using. These refrigerator pickles will keep for at least a week or two.

CHOW CHOW

This sweet and spicy relish is a Southern favorite. Try it on hamburgers, hot dogs, or alongside a meal with mashed potatoes.

YIELDS 8 CUPS

½ **head green cabbage, thinly shredded**

10 **jalapeño peppers, finely chopped (take out seeds and ribs for less heat)**

3 **red bell peppers, seeded and chopped**

3 **green bell peppers, seeded and chopped**

3 **green tomatoes, chopped**

2 **sweet onions, chopped**

⅓ **cup pickling or canning salt**

2 **cups white vinegar**

1 **cup sugar**

2 **teaspoons celery seeds**

2 **teaspoons fennel seeds**

2 **teaspoons mustard seeds**

2 **teaspoons turmeric**

1. In a large bowl, combine cabbage, jalapeños, peppers, tomatoes, and onions. Add the salt and stir well to combine. Cover and refrigerate for 6–8 hours, then rinse and drain well in a colander.

2. Put the vegetables into a large Dutch oven. Add the vinegar, sugar, celery seeds, fennel seeds, mustard seeds, and turmeric. Bring to a boil, reduce heat, and simmer until vegetables are tender but not falling apart, about 1 hour.

3. Remove vegetables from the brine, and let cool. Place in jars and store in the refrigerator. Chow Chow will keep for at least a few weeks.

Good Southern Chow

Chow Chow is mainly known as a Southern food, though a sweeter version of it is also found in Pennsylvania. It wasn't always Southern, though. Chow Chow migrated with the Acadian people after they were banished from Nova Scotia and settled in Louisiana.

FIERY PICKLED EGGS

These many sound a little odd, but they are delicious. Try them on their own as an appetizer or sliced on top of crackers or bread. Pickled eggs were once a popular bar snack, so crack a beer while you're at it.

YIELDS 6 EGGS

6 eggs

1 tablespoon pickling or canning salt

2 fresh green serrano peppers, sliced

3 garlic cloves, peeled and thinly sliced

1½ cups apple cider vinegar

½ cup water

1 teaspoon black peppercorns

1 teaspoon coriander seeds

2 whole cloves

½ teaspoon allspice

1. Hard boil the eggs by placing them in a single layer at the bottom of a pot and covering with cold water. Bring to a boil over medium-high heat, then immediately remove pot from heat and cover with lid. Let sit 12 minutes, then drain and rinse with cool water.

2. When eggs are cool enough to handle, peel them. Using a fork, gently pierce each egg through to the yolk 4 times. Place the eggs in a large, clean glass preserving jar or two smaller ones.

3. In a nonreactive saucepan, combine the remaining ingredients. Bring to a boil, then reduce heat and let simmer for 10–15 minutes. Remove from heat and let cool for a few minutes.

4. Carefully pour warm mixture over the eggs.

5. Screw the lids onto jars and refrigerate for 1 week before using. Pickled eggs will keep in the refrigerator for several weeks.

RUM CHILIES

Try these on top of fish for a little spicy, Caribbean flair. Be sure to use gloves when handling the extremely spicy Scotch Bonnet chilies.

YIELDS APPROXIMATELY 2 CUPS

1 tablespoon sugar

1 cup apple cider vinegar

2 bay leaves

1 teaspoon coriander seeds

1 teaspoon mustard seeds

1 red onion, thinly sliced

4 garlic cloves, peeled and thinly sliced

4 Scotch Bonnet chilies, stem, seeds, and ribs removed, horizontally and thinly sliced (use habaneros if you can't find Scotch Bonnets)

4 jalapeño peppers, seeds and ribs removed, thinly sliced

2 small carrots (or 1 large), thinly sliced

2 cups rum (preferably dark rum)

1. In a nonreactive saucepan, combine sugar, vinegar, bay leaves, coriander seeds, and mustard seeds. Bring to a boil, then reduce heat and let simmer for 5 minutes. Remove from heat and let cool.

2. Place onion slices, garlic, chilies, and carrots in a large, clean glass preserving jar or several smaller ones.

3. When the vinegar mixture has cooled, but is still warm, add the rum. Stir to combine, then pour mixture over chilies.

4. Screw lids on jars and store in the refrigerator for a few days before using. This spicy recipe will keep for a few weeks in the refrigerator.

Preserving in Alcohol

Besides salt and vinegar, you can also preserve chilies in alcohol. Using alcohol is one of the simplest methods of preserving because it kills bacteria. Alcohols like rum have a high sugar content so they will give the chili peppers sweetness. Try adding a dash of vodka, gin, tequila, or whiskey to a spicy pickle recipe for a more complex taste.

INDIAN MIXED GREENS

These tangy, spicy pickles are traditionally served alongside most Indian meals. Try them on their own or with flatbread.

YIELDS ABOUT 2 CUPS OF PICKLES

1 cup cauliflower, cut into small florets

2 shallots, cut horizontally into thin slices

1 large carrot, cut into thin strips

4 green jalapeño peppers, seeds and ribs removed, sliced lengthwise

1 1-inch piece of fresh ginger, peeled and sliced into thin matchsticks

1 teaspoon pickling or canning salt

½ teaspoon cayenne pepper

½ teaspoon ground turmeric

3 teaspoons fresh lime juice

2 teaspoons mustard seeds

1 teaspoon fenugreek seeds

¼ cup vegetable oil

1. Mix all the vegetables together in a large, nonreactive bowl with ginger, salt, cayenne, turmeric, and lime juice. Set aside.

2. In a spice grinder, a coffee grinder, or a mortar and pestle, blend mustard and fenugreek seeds into a fine powder. Add to vegetables and stir to combine.

3. Pack vegetables into a clean glass preserving jar. Add oil.

4. Screw lid on jar and place in the refrigerator. Let sit for 2–3 days before using. The mixed pickles will keep for a week or two in the refrigerator.

Fenugreek

Fenugreek is a plant that can be used both as a spice (the seed) and an herb (the leaves). Fenugreek is used throughout Indian and South Asian cuisine, as well as in Ethiopian and Eritrean cooking. It adds an earthy flavor to curries and sauces and can be found in most Indian and Middle Eastern markets.

PICKLED GINGER

Ginger is a wonderful root often used medicinally for digestive issues, nausea, and seasickness. The Japanese serve pickled ginger alongside raw sushi to aid in digestion. Try including a few pieces with your meals for best effect.

YIELDS APPROXIMATELY 3 CUPS

4 pounds ginger

1 tablespoon pickling or canning salt

1 cup distilled water

½ 5-gram package yogurt starter

1. Peel and cut ginger into very thin slices.
2. In a deep bowl, use a wooden mallet or the flat side of a large knife to pound ginger slices and expel juices for the brine.
3. Place juices and pounded ginger into a glass jar; mix with salt and water.
4. Add yogurt starter; seal jar.
5. Let it sit at room temperature 3–5 days, then store in refrigerator. The ginger should keep for at least a few weeks, and possibly longer.

Fermenting Tips

When fermenting foods, avoid using a plastic or an aluminum crock. This goes for your utensils as well. This goes back to the issue of reactivity that was discussed in Part I. Instead, be sure to use glass or enamel pottery specifically meant for making sauerkraut and pickles.

THAI VEGETABLES

These pickled vegetables are great as a side dish, a snack, or on top of a bed of greens. The longer they sit in the marinade, the spicier and more vinegary they will get.

YIELDS APPROXIMATELY 6 CUPS

4 cloves garlic, peeled and minced

6 dried red chilies, seeded and crumbled

3 tablespoons chopped green onion

1 tablespoon fresh grated ginger

2–3 tablespoons vegetable oil

3½ cups rice wine vinegar

1 tablespoon sugar

¼ cup chopped lemongrass

4 cups water

1 cup baby corn

1 cup sliced carrots

1 cup broccoli florets

½ cup bok choy

1 large cucumber, seeded and cut into 3-inch-long, ½-inch wide strips

½ cup cilantro leaves

2–3 tablespoons toasted sesame seeds

1. Place the garlic, chilies, green onions, and ginger in a food processor or blender and process to form a paste. Heat the oil in a wok or frying pan, add the paste, and stir-fry for 4–5 minutes. Remove from heat and allow the mixture to cool to room temperature.

2. In a small saucepan, bring the vinegar to a boil. Add the sugar and the lemongrass; reduce heat and simmer for 20 minutes. Stir in the reserved paste, set aside. This will serve as the marinade.

3. Bring the water to a boil in a large pan. Add the corn, carrots, broccoli, and bok choy and blanch for 2–3 minutes. Strain the vegetables and shock with cool water to stop the cooking process.

4. Place the vegetables in a large bowl and pour the marinade over the top. Let cool to room temperature and then refrigerate for at least 4 hours or up to 2 weeks.

5. Stir in the cilantro and sesame seeds just before serving.

QUICK-PICKLED
SESAME BROCCOLINI

This recipe uses upscale broccolini as the base for a quick pickled snack that's perfect for parties.

YIELDS APPROXIMATELY 1 PINT

1 pound of broccolini (approximately 1 large bunch)

1 teaspoon pickling or canning salt

2 garlic cloves, peeled and minced

2 tablespoons rice wine vinegar

⅛ teaspoon cayenne pepper

2 tablespoons sesame oil

1. Peel any overly-thick broccolini stems so that they are all the same thickness, and trim any excessively long stems.
2. Toss the broccolini with the remaining ingredients in a small bowl. Cover the bowl, and place it in the refrigerator for up to 2 days.
3. Drain the broccolini and reheat in a pan to serve the stalks alongside a stir-fry, or as a topping to steamed white rice.

TRADITIONAL
KOREAN KIMCHI

Variations of kimchi emphasize radishes, scallions, or cucumbers, and seasoning options include ginger, chocolate, and coffee.

YIELDS APPROXIMATELY 4 PINTS

4 cloves garlic, peeled

1 cup onion, chopped

2 tablespoons diced gingerroot

1 tablespoon unpasteurized miso

4 heads green cabbage

½ daikon radish

3 tablespoons pickling or canning salt

1. Using a food processor, blender, or heavy-duty juicer, blend the garlic, onion, ginger, and miso into a sauce.
2. Grate, shred, or chop the cabbage and daikon radish. Mix in the salt and squeeze or pound the cabbage to create the brine.
3. Mix the cabbage and daikon with the kimchi sauce.
4. Pack the kimchi into a 1-gallon glass jar or crock. Make sure there are no gaps or air pockets. Place a weight over the kimchi to keep it covered in the brine. Place a lid loosely over the opening so pressure may still release.
5. Let the kimchi sit at room temperature. It will be ready to eat in 4–5 days. Place in smaller glass jars, seal them, and store in the refrigerator for up to a month.

Kimchi

This Korean dish dates back thousands of years and is first mentioned in Chinese writings that date to about 1000 B.C.E. Kimchi is a good source of probiotics, vitamin A, and vitamin C.

HOT and PUNGENT KIMCHI

This version of kimchi is downright potent, funky, fiery, and probably not for everyone. Still, for those who crave authentic flavor, this recipe can't be beat!

YIELDS 20 SERVINGS

1 head of napa cabbage (about 2 pounds)

6 tablespoons pickling or canning salt

1 small daikon radish, cut into thin matchsticks

2 tablespoons ground Korean red chilies (you should be able to find this at most Asian groceries; if not use red chili pepper flakes)

2 tablespoons diced Thai red chilies

2 tablespoons sugar

4 cloves of garlic, peeled and finely minced

½ bunch scallions, finely chopped

1 (2-inch) piece of fresh ginger, peeled and finely minced

4 tablespoons fish sauce, available at Asian markets

3 tablespoons salted shrimp paste (available at Asian markets)

1. Slicing lengthwise, cut the cabbage into quarters. Working carefully, sprinkle the quarters with 3 tablespoons of the salt, being sure to get salt in between all the layers of leaves.

2. Toss daikon with remaining salt in a large bowl. Add cabbage and let vegetables sit for at least 2 hours.

3. After a few hours, the cabbage should be quite wilted. Put cabbage and daikon in a colander to drain liquid. Rinse well, making sure to get all the salt out from in between the leaves. Shake gently to dry.

4. Combine the rest of the ingredients into a paste, making sure to avoid inhaling peppers or rubbing your eyes and mouth while handling the paste.

5. Rub the paste all over the vegetables, again getting inside all of the layers of cabbage leaves. Pack the kimchi into a large, clean glass preserving jar or several smaller ones. You may need to cut the cabbage into smaller sections to do so.

6. Screw the lid on the jars and let kimchi sit out for 24 hours before refrigerating.

7. Move kimchi to the refrigerator, using as needed. It will continue to ferment in the refrigerator, getting even tastier and more sour. It will keep for at least a week.

UME RADISH PICKLES

These pickles can be made ahead of time, and then stored in the refrigerator for a week. Because umeboshi vinegar turns vegetables pink, these pickles add a splash of bright pink color to the plate. Other root vegetables, greens, or red cabbage can be used in place of radishes.

YIELDS 1 CUP

4 small red radishes

¾ cup water

¼ cup umeboshi vinegar

1. Slice radishes into thin half-moons.
2. Place sliced radishes into a glass jar.
3. Pour umeboshi vinegar and water over radishes.
4. Cover jar with a cheesecloth and store at room temperature for 1–3 days.
5. Rinse off the liquid before serving.

Quick Pickles

Pickles that can be made in one to three days are considered to be quick pickles. They are generally lighter and sweeter than preserved pickles, and they are best served in warmer weather, such as spring and summer. A quick dip in umeboshi vinegar will turn any mild vegetable into a colorful and vibrant-tasting condiment for an Asian-style meal.

DAIKON and CARROT TAMARI PRESERVES

Tamari quick pickles use tamari as the fermenting agent. Regular soy sauce can also be used in place of tamari. A variety of root vegetables can also be used for pickling.

YIELDS 1 CUP

½ **medium carrot**
½ **medium daikon**
½ **cup tamari**
1½ **cups water**

1. Slice carrot and daikon into matchsticks, keeping the size and shape as even as possible.
2. Place carrot and daikon strips into a glass jar.
3. Cover vegetables with tamari and water.
4. Cover the jar with a cheesecloth and store at room temperature for 1–3 days.
5. Rinse off the salty liquid before serving.

Tamari

Tamari is a traditional Japanese variety of soy sauce that tends to be thicker and more deeply flavored than the traditional soy that you see in grocery stores. Because of this, it tends to impart a more complex taste than other varieties. You should be able to find at least one kind of tamari at your local grocery store. If not, any Asian grocer will have multiple varieties available.

BURMESE-STYLE
MUSTARD GREENS

This type of blend is very popular throughout Asia and the Eastern world as an appetizer, side dish, or snack. Try it with Chinese five-spice powder in place of the ginger.

YIELDS 2 QUARTS

1½ pounds mustard greens

3 cups carrots, thinly sliced

½ pound shallots, peeled

2 fresh red chilies, seeded and diced

2 teaspoons pickling or canning salt

2 teaspoons brown sugar

1 teaspoon fresh ginger, grated

⅓ cup dark ale

⅔ cup malt vinegar

1. Thoroughly rinse the mustard greens; blanch in boiling water for 30 seconds and dunk in an ice bath. Dry the greens, and then cut into ¼-inch slices.

2. Mix the remaining ingredients in a large bowl; add the greens and turn to coat evenly.

3. Cover with a plate for weight; secure with plastic wrap. Let sit for 24 hours. Greens can be refrigerated, frozen, or canned. Flavor improves with aging. If canning, pack to within 1 inch of a quart container, secure the lid, and put in a hot water bath for 15 minutes. Test lids when cool. Greens that are canned will last for at least several months in a cold place, while noncanned greens should be used within a week or two.

PICKLED CHINESE CABBAGE

This pickled cabbage is a relative to Korean kimchi, although its process is quicker, its flavor is milder, and the pickling agent is rice vinegar, not merely salt and cabbage liquid.

YIELDS 3 POUNDS

4 cups water

6 cups rice vinegar

1 tablespoon chopped garlic

1 tablespoon chopped cilantro

2 large shallots (or 1 medium onion), chopped

3 pounds Chinese cabbage, cored, halved, and thinly sliced

Salt to taste

White pepper to taste

1. Place water, vinegar, garlic, cilantro, and shallots in a large stew pot and bring to a boil. Reduce heat and simmer for 5 minutes.
2. Bring the cooking liquid back to a boil and stir in the cabbage. Cover and cook the cabbage for 3–5 minutes.
3. Remove the pot from heat and let cool to room temperature. Season to taste with salt and white pepper.
4. Refrigerate for at least 8 hours before serving. This cabbage will last for a week or so in the refrigerator.

SWEET PICKLED FIGS

Be sure to get firm, ripe figs for this recipe. If they're too ripe, they turn to mush when cooking. When you serve these, warm them up in a low oven and top with some ricotta cheese.

YIELDS APPROXIMATELY 3 PINTS

1 cup sugar

½ cup honey

4 cups water

2½ pounds fresh ripe figs, peeled and quartered

2 cups red wine vinegar

2 (¼-inch) slices ginger

1 tablespoon whole cloves

1. Combine sugar, honey, and water in a medium saucepan. Bring to a boil.
2. Add the figs to the boiling sugar-water mixture, lower the heat, and simmer for 20 minutes.
3. Add remaining ingredients to mixture, and continue cooking gently for another 20 minutes. Let the mixture cool down.
4. Place the mixture into sterilized pint-sized glass jars, cover, and process in a boiling water bath for 15 minutes. The processed figs will keep for at least several months in a cold place.

CRANBERRY-RASPBERRY SAUCE

This is a unique adaptation of a Thanksgiving favorite that's yummy all year, but specifically designed to be frozen for holiday storage. Think how easy it will be to make this weeks ahead of time!

YIELDS APPROXIMATELY 5–6 CUPS

1¼ cups sugar

½ cup raspberry vinegar

¼ cup water

1 (12-ounce) package fresh cranberries

1 cup fresh raspberries

1 cinnamon stick

¼-inch piece vanilla bean

1 tablespoon thinly sliced orange peel

1. Combine sugar, raspberry vinegar, and water in a large nonreactive pan over medium heat; bring to a boil, stirring constantly until sugar dissolves.

2. Add cranberries, raspberries, cinnamon stick, vanilla bean, and orange peel.

3. Reduce heat to low; cover partially and simmer 10 minutes, or until cranberries burst.

4. Remove from heat; take out the cinnamon stick and cool completely.

5. Place in freezer-safe containers, leaving ½-inch headspace. The sauce can be kept in the freezer for several months. Thaw in fridge for 24–48 hours before serving.

QUICK PINEAPPLE PICKLES

This quick pickle is flavored with warming spices, and, like Cranberry-Raspberry Sauce, makes a wonderful addition to a holiday condiment platter.

YIELDS APPROXIMATELY 1 QUART

¼ cup apple cider

⅓ cup apple cider vinegar

½ cup pineapple juice

3 tablespoons brown sugar

1 tablespoon honey

1 teaspoon nutmeg

2 cinnamon sticks

4 cups diced fresh pineapple

1. In a medium saucepan, bring the cider, cider vinegar, pineapple juice, sugar, honey, and spices to a boil over medium heat, stirring constantly.
2. Once the sugar is dissolved, turn off the heat and let the mixture cool slightly.
3. Place the pineapple chunks in either a large canning jar or a large heatproof bowl, and pour the vinegar mixture over them.
4. Place the pickles in the refrigerator for at least 24 hours. These quick pickles will keep for at least a week.

WATERMELON PICKLES

This is a Southern favorite that has a fresh, thirst-quenching quality.

YIELDS 5 PINTS

4 pounds watermelon rind

½ cup pickling or canning salt

8 cups water

4 cups sugar

2 cups white vinegar

5 (½-inch) cinnamon sticks

10 whole cloves

5 (¼-inch) slices ginger, peeled

1 lemon, sliced into 5 pieces

1. Trim the pink parts off the watermelon rind; cube rind.
2. Soak the rind in pickling salt and water overnight; drain and rinse thoroughly.
3. Place rind in a large pot and cover with water; simmer until tender, being careful not to overcook.
4. In a large stockpot, mix remaining ingredients; simmer 10 minutes.
5. Add watermelon rind, cooking over low heat until nearly transparent.
6. Transfer rind and liquid to ½-pint jars. Leave ½-inch headspace; process in hot-water bath 10 minutes. The pickles will last for at least several months in a cold place.

PICKLED PEACHES

Pickled peaches are a wonderful summertime dish and go exceptionally well with a variety of grilled meats, as well as in hearty salads.

YIELDS 4 QUARTS

5 cups sugar

2½ cups white vinegar

2½ cups water

4 cinnamon sticks

8 whole cloves

4 (¼-inch) slices fresh ginger

12 cups peaches, peeled and pitted

1. Combine sugar, vinegar, water, and spices; bring to a boil.
2. Let the mixture boil for 30 seconds, then add the fruit. Adjust the heat to a low boil, and cook the fruit until partly tender, approximately 5 minutes.
3. Pack fruit into sterilized jars, pouring syrup over top and leaving ½-inch headspace.
4. Add tops; process 10 minutes in hot water bath. These peaches can last for a year under cold conditions.

Just Peachy

Peaches had their beginning in China, where they were favored by the royal family. They appear in Chinese writings dating to the tenth century B.C.E. Peaches traveled with Persian merchants, who introduced them to Europe. Peaches were one of the fruits brought to America by the Spanish in the seventeenth century.

SPICED ORANGE RINGS

These look beautiful in a gift basket, and they taste great, too!

YIELDS 4 PINTS

6 large oranges

1½ cups granulated sugar

1½ cups white vinegar

4 (2-inch) cinnamon sticks

2 teaspoons whole cloves

1 teaspoon whole allspice berries

1. Wash oranges. Cut into ¼-inch slices; seed.
2. Place oranges in a heavy pan; cover with cold water. Heat to boiling. Lower heat; simmer until fruit is tender, about 45 minutes. Drain in a colander.
3. Heat sugar, vinegar, cinnamon, cloves, and allspice berries until boiling. Add orange rings a few at a time; cook at a moderate boil until rings are tender and clear, about 15 minutes.
4. Remove the orange slices and the whole spices from the syrup. Pack orange slices in sterilized pint jars, leaving ¼-inch headspace. Divide spices evenly between 4 jars.
5. Ladle hot syrup over orange slices, leaving ¼-inch headspace. Wipe rims; cap and seal.
6. Process in water-bath canner 10 minutes. The canned oranges will keep for up to a year. As always, keeping them in a cold place will prolong their shelf life.

Oranges Arrive

It was 1493 when Christopher Columbus brought orange seeds to Haiti; they eventually made it from Haiti into Florida in the early sixteenth century. The most popular oranges are sweet oranges, which come in navel, Valencia, Persian, and blood orange varieties.

PRESERVED LEMONS

Preserving lemons does magical things to their flavor. Take the preserved skin of the lemons, chop it finely, and add it to Mediterranean or Middle Eastern dishes. Much as in sauerkraut or kimchi, these pickles are cured only in salt—the liquid from the lemons does the rest.

YIELDS APPROXIMATELY 1 QUART

8 large lemons, or 10 Meyer lemons

½ cup pickling or canning salt

4–5 sprigs fresh rosemary

½ teaspoon whole black peppercorns (optional)

1. Cut each lemon open by making two intersecting cuts ¾ of the way through the fruit. You should be able to open the lemon up like a flower petal.

2. Generously coat all the surfaces of the lemons with the pickling salt.

3. Place the lemons into a sterilized quart-sized glass jar, compressing them as you go. You're aiming to create a substantial amount of lemon juice in the jar, so don't handle them delicately.

4. Add more salt and lemon juice to cover, if necessary. Add the rosemary sprigs and the peppercorns, if using.

5. Cap the jar, and allow it to stay at room temperature for two days before moving it to the refrigerator. Let the lemons soften for 3 weeks, occasionally shaking the jar to make sure that the juice reaches all of the lemons.

6. To use, remove a lemon, rinse the salt off, and then utilize the skin in your recipe. The lemons will keep in the jar for 4–6 months.

PICKLED LIMES

Pickled limes are one of the easier fruit pickles to make, similar to preserved lemons. Pickled limes can also be a spicy pickle, which is a staple of some South Asian cuisines.

YIELDS APPROXIMATELY 1 PINT

1 quart water

½ cup pickling or canning salt

6 medium limes, cut into quarters

1. In a medium saucepan, bring the water to a boil. Meanwhile, sterilize your canning jar(s).
2. Once the water is boiling, add the pickling salt, and stir to dissolve. Once the salt is no longer visible, shut off the heat and allow the brine to cool slightly
3. Pack the limes down into your sanitized jar, adding the rest of the ingredients. Pour the brine over the limes and make sure that they are totally submerged before you cap the jar.
4. Cap the jar, and allow it to stay at room temperature for two days before moving it to the refrigerator. Let the limes soften for at least a week. To use them, rinse off the salt, and then either dice the flesh or use the skins to add deep flavor to a number of dishes.

CANNED APPLES

Pickled apples are wonderful in cold weather—they seem to capture all of the warm essence of a crisp fall day, but with an underlying tartness from the pickling solution. Truly gourmet territory.

YIELDS APPROXIMATELY 1 QUART

8 medium-sized firm apples

1 cup apple cider vinegar

½ cup red wine vinegar

½ cup white vinegar

3½ cups sugar

1 tablespoon cloves

1 tablespoon allspice berries

1 stick cinnamon

1. Clean, peel, and quarter the apples, removing the core and the seeds.

2. Heat the vinegars and sugar in a medium saucepan to a rolling boil. Add the loose spices. (You may tie the spices in a small cheesecloth pouch for easier removal.)

3. Add the quartered apples to the pickling mixture. Turn down the heat to a straight simmer, and cook until the apples are quite tender and easily pierced with the tip of a knife, approximately 10 minutes.

4. Remove the apples to a sterile quart-sized glass jar.

5. Continue cooking the vinegar mixture down until it takes the consistency of a syrup. Pour the mixture over the apples in the jar. Cap and refrigerate, using the apples within a few weeks.

QUICK-PICKLED PLUMS

These plums are pickled with a sweet and spicy mixture of vinegar and warming spices. They are a fantastic accompaniment to any grilled meat, with their sweet and sour flavor profile. This recipe is designed to be used within a week or so. If you'd like your pickles to last longer, process the jars in a boiling water bath for 10 minutes.

YIELDS APPROXIMATELY 1 QUART

8 firm plums, any variety

1 cup red wine vinegar

1 cup apple cider vinegar

2 cups water

2 cups sugar

2 teaspoons whole cloves

1 teaspoon allspice berries

1. Slice plums into wedges or dice them into large rectangles. Place them into a sterilized quart-sized canning jar.

2. In a medium saucepan, bring the vinegars, water, and sugar to a boil, making sure the sugar is fully dissolved. Once the liquid reaches a boil, add the cloves and allspice berries (you may use a small cheesecloth bag to keep the seasonings together). Simmer for 5 minutes.

3. Remove the allspice and cloves, and then pour the hot liquid over the plums in the canning jars. Cool mixture to room temperature before covering and placing in the fridge. Allow the flavors to mingle overnight. Use the plums within a week or two.

REFRIGERATOR HERRING

This is a common side dish and snack in Scandinavia during Christmas and midsummer celebrations.

YIELDS 2 POUNDS

2 pounds salt herring fillets

¾ cup water

½ cup white vinegar

⅓ cup red wine vinegar

1 bay leaf

¼ teaspoon black peppercorns

¼ teaspoon whole allspice berries

¼ teaspoon dill seeds

½ cinnamon stick

⅓ cup granulated sugar

1 red onion

1. Soak fillets in water in refrigerator 6 hours; change water and soak 6 hours more. Rinse and slice into bite-sized pieces.
2. In a saucepan, combine remaining ingredients except onion; boil for 5 minutes, stirring regularly.
3. Slice onion; layer into jars with fish.
4. Add pickling mixture and cap. Let age about 1 week before serving. Use within 3 weeks.

A Red Herring?

Herrings live in temperate shallow waters in the North Atlantic. The term "a red herring" came about because of the potent smell of red herrings. Fox hunters could divert their competition by dragging herring across the good trail, confusing the opponents' hounds.

SAUERBRATEN

This pickled beef is traditionally served with potatoes, dumplings, or cabbage.

YIELDS 4 POUNDS

MARINADE

1 cup red wine

1 cup red wine vinegar

2 cups water

1 onion, sliced

1 tablespoon crushed peppercorn

1 tablespoon crushed juniper berries

2 bay leaves

1 teaspoon mustard seeds

1 teaspoon pickling salt

1 teaspoon freshly grated ginger

MEAT

1 (3–4-pound) bottom round

BRAISING SAUCE

1½ tablespoons butter

2 cups red onion, diced

1½ cups diced celery

2 cups diced carrots

4 tablespoons flour

Water, as needed

1. Place ingredients for marinade in a large saucepan; boil 10 minutes. Cool.

2. Find a large container that will hold the beef and marinade. Marinate in refrigerator 3 days, turning meat regularly.

3. Drain meat, straining marinade. Put marinade aside.

4. In a covered oven dish, heat butter; brown meat on all sides. Roast with the reserved marinade at 350°F for 1¼ hours, uncovered.

5. Meanwhile, toss vegetables lightly in flour; add to the oven dish after 2 hours. Continue cooking the roast for another hour, or until cooked to an internal temperature of 140°F. If the vegetables are browning too quickly, remove them from the roasting pan. If you are in danger of running out of marinade at any point, you may add water to prevent the juices from reducing too much.

6. Remove the roast from the oven, let rest for 10 minutes, and then serve.

PICKLED SHRIMP

These lightly pickled shellfish make a delightfully different appetizer for a summer party. Serve them with fruit for a refreshing and light first course to a Southern dinner.

YIELDS APPROXIMATELY 1 QUART

2 pounds fresh shrimp, peeled

4 cloves garlic, peeled

2 white onions, sliced

1 tablespoon peppercorns

1 teaspoon red pepper flakes

½ cup apple cider vinegar

½ cup white wine vinegar

1. Fill a large stockpot with cold water and bring to a boil over medium-high heat. Have a large bowl of ice water nearby.

2. When the water comes to a boil, add the shrimp, and cook until opaque, about 5 minutes. Transfer the shrimp to the ice water to halt the cooking process, and then drain them.

3. Place the cooled shrimp, along with the garlic, onion, and seasonings, into your sterilized quart-sized canning jar.

4. Pour the vinegars over the shrimp, cap the jar, and shake gently to mix.

5. Refrigerate the shrimp at least overnight, and for up to 10 days.

PART III

MEALS
WITH
PICKLES

Now that you've added a number of pickle recipes to your repertoire, it's time to expand your culinary horizons by utilizing your pickles in the sides, condiments, and entrées that you'll be making. Improvisation is key in cooking with pickles. Ideally, the strong flavors of your preserved ingredients—whether they're salty, sour, sweet, or fiery—should work as either a counterpoint or a complement to the tastes of your primary ingredients. There are no right or wrong ways to use your pickles, but it's important to always taste your food as you're going along, including your pickles, as this will help you properly balance and season the dish you're creating. Correctly handled, these dishes will shine with the nuanced but unmistakable taste of pickled ingredients that never overpower the main focus of the recipe. Enjoy, experiment, and have fun!

Hummus with Sweet Minted Eggplant, see Part III

Condiments, Starters, and Salads

PICKLED ONION SAUCE

This is an intense onion sauce that marries nicely with bratwurst, garlic sausage, and kielbasa. Other herbs worth trying in this blend include cumin, ginger, and allspice.

YIELDS 3 CUPS

2 chili peppers, seeded and diced

1 cup Sweet Red Onions (see Part II)

10 cloves fresh garlic, peeled

1½ cups white vinegar

½ cup sugar

1 tablespoon mustard seeds

1 tablespoon celery seeds

½ cup dark beer

¼ cup dark honey

1 teaspoon pickling or canning salt

1. Blanch peppers in boiling water for 2 minutes.
2. Place Sweet Red Onions, peppers, and remaining ingredients in a saucepan; bring to a boil.
3. Reduce heat; simmer until sauce reduces by ¼ cup.
4. Cool; run through a blender or food processor for consistent texture.
5. Store in freezer-safe containers, leaving space for expansion. Use within 8 months.

PICKLED GINGER SAUCE

This is a wonderful Asian-style dipping sauce that can be canned or frozen. If you don't have find enough pickled ginger juice, many stores carry regular ginger juice.

YIELDS 2 CUPS

½ cup rice wine vinegar

¼ cup fresh lime juice

1 tablespoon dried onion flakes

½ tablespoon chives

1 teaspoon freshly ground pepper

1½ teaspoons Pickled Ginger (see Part II), minced, plus 1 cup juice, from the pickles.

1 teaspoon soy sauce

2 tablespoons chopped green onion, for garnish

1. Mix all the ingredients together in a non-aluminum pan over medium heat.

2. Let the sauce come to a low rolling boil; drop the heat to a simmer, and slowly reduce by about ½ cup.

3. Cool and preserve. Add green onion when serving.

HUMMUS with SWEET MINTED EGGPLANT

This is a delicious hummus made with garbanzo beans and aromatic eggplant pickles. Inspect the garbanzos after soaking and discard any that are still hard. This recipe is delicious as a spread or a dip for crackers, or as a condiment on a gyro or falafel.

YIELDS APPROXIMATELY 2 CUPS

1 cup canned garbanzo beans

¼ cup tahini paste

1 clove garlic, peeled and minced

¼ cup lemon juice

2 tablespoons Sweet Minted Eggplant, minced
   (see Part II)

½ teaspoon cumin

½ teaspoon salt

¼ cup olive oil, as needed for consistency

1. Soak the garbanzo beans in 5 cups water for 12 hours. Drain and rinse.
2. In a food processor with an *S* blade, process all ingredients except the olive oil. Gradually add the olive oil until the mixture becomes creamy.

Garbanzo Beans

Garbanzo beans, also called chickpeas, are the traditional ingredient in hummus and falafel. They are a great source of protein and fiber and are high in folic acid as well as the minerals molybdenum, manganese, copper, phosphorus, and iron. Garbanzos originated in the Middle East, where they are a staple food.

SPRING ROLLS

Both barbecued pork and chicken marinated in oyster sauce also work well in this recipe.

YIELDS 12 SPRING ROLLS

½ pound pork tenderloin, diced

2 tablespoons oyster sauce, divided

½ teaspoon baking soda

6 dried mushrooms

1 tablespoon chicken broth or stock

½ teaspoon sugar

3½ tablespoons oil, divided

1 cup mung bean sprouts, rinsed and drained

¼ cup Pickled Carrots, julienned (see Part II)

¼ cup Ume Radish Pickles, julienned (see Part II)

2 green onions, thinly sliced on the diagonal

¼ teaspoon sesame oil

4–6 cups oil for frying

12 spring roll wrappers

2 tablespoons cornstarch mixed with 1 tablespoon water

1. Marinate the pork in 1 tablespoon oyster sauce and baking soda for 30 minutes.
2. Soak the dried mushrooms in hot water to soften; drain and thinly slice.
3. Combine the remaining 1 tablespoon oyster sauce, chicken broth, and sugar to form sauce. Set aside.
4. Add 2 tablespoons oil to a preheated wok or skillet. When oil is hot, add the pork. Stir-fry briefly until it changes color and is nearly cooked through. Remove from the wok.
5. Add 1½ tablespoons oil. When oil is hot, add the dried mushrooms. Stir-fry for 1 minute, then add the bean sprouts, Pickled Carrot, Radish Pickles, and the green onion. Add the sauce in the middle of the wok and bring to a boil. Add the pork and mix through. Drizzle with the sesame oil. Cool.
6. Heat 4–6 cups oil to 375°F. While oil is heating, prepare the spring rolls. To wrap, lay the wrapper in a diamond shape. Place a tablespoon of filling in the middle. Coat all the edges with the cornstarch-and-water mixture. Roll up the wrapper and tuck in the edges. Seal the tucked-in edges with cornstarch and water. Continue with the remainder of the spring rolls. (Prepare more cornstarch and water as necessary.)
7. In a large, deep-sided pan or wok, deep-fry the spring rolls, two at a time, until they turn golden. Drain on paper towels.

HALIBUT CEVICHE
with RED ONIONS

Ceviche is a casual yet classy Latin appetizer of raw fish that has been briefly firmed up by its contact with citrus juice. The flavors of your pickles will really shine through against this delectable backdrop. Ceviche is not cooked, so make sure to use only the freshest fish, and do not serve this to anyone who doesn't like sushi!

YIELDS 4 SERVINGS

1½ pounds fresh halibut

½ cup lime juice

2 Vinegar-Packed Peppers (see Part II)

1 large red tomato

4 tablespoons fresh cilantro

¼ cup Sweet Red Onions (see Part II)

½ cup orange juice

1 teaspoon salt

1. Cut the halibut into ½-inch cubes. Combine the fish and lime juice in a small glass or ceramic container. Cover and refrigerate for 1 hour.

2. Dice the Vingar-Packed Peppers into ¼-inch pieces. Chop the tomato into ¼-inch pieces; reserve the juice. Chop the cilantro into ¼-inch pieces.

3. Drain off and discard the lime juice and put the fish in a medium-sized mixing bowl. Add the Sweet Red Onions, Vinegar-Packed Peppers, tomatoes with their juice, cilantro, orange juice, and salt; stir well. Refrigerate in a glass or ceramic container for 4 to 12 hours.

BRUSCHETTA with RED PEPPER and ARTICHOKE HEARTS

This recipe is a perfect marriage of strong Mediterranean flavors. The deep, smoky pepper will work wonders with the piquant artichoke hearts.

YIELDS 6 SERVINGS

3 red peppers

1 teaspoon extra-virgin olive oil

1 teaspoon balsamic vinegar

¼ bunch fresh oregano, chopped

12 (1½-inch-thick) slices baguette

1½ ounces Manchego cheese (Romano or Parmesan can be substituted)

Fresh-cracked black pepper, to taste

12 Spiced Artichoke Hearts (see Part II)

1. Preheat oven to 400°F.
2. Coat the red peppers with a bit of the oil and place on a baking sheet; roast until the skin blisters, approximately 10 minutes. Remove the peppers from the oven and immediately place in a sealed plastic bag; let sit for a minimum of 5 minutes. Remove the peppers from the bag and peel off and discard the skin.
3. Purée the peppers in a blender, then add the vinegar and continue to process into a smooth paste. Mix in the chopped oregano. Let stand for at least 1 hour (can be prepared a day in advance and refrigerated).
4. Use a pastry brush to coat the bread slices lightly with the remaining oil. Toast until lightly golden brown.
5. Spread the puréed pepper on the toasted bread and sprinkle with cheese and black pepper. Top each slice with a Spiced Artichoke Heart.

PECAN and GOAT CHEESE SALAD

This quick salad has a rich flavor that works in large portions as a side for a pasta dish or in small portions as an appetizer. The pleasant sweet and sour flavor of the pickled beets works well to offset the richness of the goat cheese and nuts.

YIELDS 4 SERVINGS

4 cups mixed baby greens

2 tablespoons Italian salad dressing

½ cup goat cheese, crumbled

½ cup diced Sweet and Sour Beets (see Part II)

⅔ cup pecans, chopped

Mix greens and dressing together in a medium salad bowl. Toss well to coat. Add goat cheese, pickled beets, and pecans to salad. Toss to mix and serve immediately.

ASIAN CHOPPED SALAD with CRISPY NOODLES and KIMCHI

If you haven't made your own kimchi, you can buy it at any Asian grocer. Remember that kimchi can pack quite a kick, so you may want to use it sparingly until you get a handle on its potency.

YIELDS 4 SERVINGS

2 bunches scallions, trimmed and thinly sliced

8 ounces tofu, diced

2 cups baby spinach

1 cup water chestnuts, chopped

1 cup crispy chow mein noodles, crumbled

1 cup fresh shelled edamame

½ cup Traditional Korean Kimchi (see Part II), drained and chopped

½ cup chopped baby corn

2 tablespoons toasted sesame seeds

Asian-style commercial salad dressing, to taste

Combine all the ingredients in a large salad bowl.

Add chosen dressing to taste and toss to coat.

Serve immediately.

Chow Mein and Baby Corn?

Chow mein noodles are deep-fried until crispy and add a zesty crunch to any salad mixture, but particularly to one that is Asian inspired. The baby corn that often turns up in Chinese stir-fries is corn that is harvested early just after the silk is produced. The tiny cobs retain crispiness while adding a sweet undertone to other dishes. These are readily available canned.

BULGUR SALAD with ROASTED CHICKPEAS and LEMON

Bulgur is whole pieces of wheat that have been cleaned, parboiled, dried, and sorted into sizes. It's healthier than rice or pasta, and just as easy.

YIELDS 4 SERVINGS

1¼ cups water

1 cup coarse bulgur

Pinch of salt

1 medium red onion, thinly sliced

2 tablespoons olive oil

Juice from 1 lemon

2 bay leaves

1 teaspoon cumin seeds

½ teaspoon ground turmeric

½ teaspoon ground paprika

Pinch of cayenne pepper

1 (15-ounce) can chickpeas, rinsed and drained

2 tablespoons Brined Capers (see Part II)

Additional salt to taste

Pepper to taste

1. Bring the water to a boil in a saucepan and add the bulgur and a pinch of salt. Turn off the heat, and let it sit, uncovered, for 20 minutes until all of the water has been absorbed.
2. Preheat the oven to 400°F.
3. Place an ovenproof skillet over medium heat. Once it is heated, add the onion, oil, lemon juice, bay leaves, cumin, turmeric, paprika, and cayenne. Stir until the onions are coated with the spices. Cook the onions for 5–7 minutes until they're soft and the spices smell toasted. Stir the chickpeas into the onions and cook until they start to sizzle. Add the Brined Capers.
4. Place the skillet into the middle of the oven for 20 minutes and stir halfway through. Remove the skillet from the oven, discard the bay leaves, and season with salt and pepper as necessary. Gently reheat the bulgur, pour the contents of the skillet over it, and serve hot.

CELLOPHANE NOODLE SALAD

In the traditional Thai version of this salad, cooks use fish sauce instead of soy sauce and use ground pork, shrimp, and/or chicken for the meat. Thais also are likely to use dried "rat dropping" chilies that they crumble into the bowl. Mighty hot.

YIELDS 4 SERVINGS

4 ounces cellophane, or bean thread, noodles, softened in hot water for 20 minutes

1 (6-ounce) package soy "chicken" strips, optional

½ cup thinly sliced scallions

½ cup fresh cilantro leaves

1–2 tablespoons crushed red peppers

2 tablespoons lime juice

2 tablespoons soy sauce

1 tablespoon chopped Pungent Pickled Garlic (see Part II)

Sugar to taste

1. Drain the softened noodles and cut them into serving pieces. Put the noodles, "chicken" strips if using, scallions, cilantro leaves, and crushed red peppers into a serving bowl.

2. Mix together the lime juice, soy sauce, and pickled garlic and toss with the salad ingredients, add sugar to taste, then serve.

What Are Cellophane Noodles?

Called "glass," "cellophane," or "bean thread" noodles, this Asian pasta is made from the starch of mung beans, and when dried, the noodles are so brittle and tough that when you cut them—and the cleanest way is using scissors—they may fly around, so hold them over the sink. They are easier to cut when wet, although when they are wet they are also somewhat gelatinous. Unless you plan to use the softened noodles in a soup, drain them before using them in other dishes.

Entrées

HOMEMADE
REUBEN PANINI

You could also make this panini with corned beef. Pumpernickel bread is another option that you should try.

YIELDS 1 SERVING

5 slices pastrami

2 slices Swiss cheese

2 slices rye bread

¼ cup Sauerkraut (see Part II)

2 tablespoons Russian dressing

1. Preheat a panini press. Pile the pastrami and Swiss cheese onto 1 slice of bread. Top with Sauerkraut, and then spread the Russian dressing on the other piece of rye bread before placing on top of the Sauerkraut.

2. Place on panini press, close lid, and cook for 3–5 minutes.

3. Remove from press, cut in half, and serve warm.

Reuben or Rachel?

In the case of these two closely linked deli sandwiches, it's actually the pickle itself that usually defines which is which. A Reuben is a pastrami or corned beef sandwich with sauerkraut, while a Rachel has coleslaw.

MEDITERRANEAN
QUINOA PILAF

If you can't find quinoa at your local grocery store, you can substitute couscous. Quinoa is a grain, but couscous, like pasta, is made from semolina flour. Follow the cooking times on the package when making this recipe.

YIELDS 2 SERVINGS

1 tablespoon olive oil

½ small onion, chopped

¼ teaspoon ground cinnamon

½ teaspoon ground coriander

½ teaspoon ground turmeric

Pinch red chili flakes

1 cup vegetable broth

1 small garlic clove, peeled and minced

½ cup quinoa

½ can red kidney beans, rinsed and drained

½ can black beans, rinsed and drained

1 Roma tomato, chopped

2 tablespoons chopped Preserved Lemons (see Part II)

Salt and pepper to taste

1. Place a skillet over medium heat. Once it is heated, add the olive oil and onion. Cook for 5–7 minutes, stirring occasionally. The onion should be soft and just starting to turn golden. Add the cinnamon, coriander, turmeric, and chili flakes. Stir continually for 1 minute and then add the vegetable broth.

2. Use your spatula to loosen any spices or onion that may have stuck to the skillet. Add the garlic, quinoa, and beans. Reduce the heat to low, cover the skillet, and simmer for 15 minutes. The water should be mostly absorbed.

3. Add the tomato and Preserved Lemons. Stir and cook for 5 more minutes, or until the water is evaporated, season with salt and pepper to taste. Fluff with a fork and serve immediately.

PIQUANT BEEF CHOW FUN

Barbecued pork also works well in this dish. The pickled mustard greens add an extra something special to this savory recipe for an interesting juxtaposition of color and texture.

YIELDS 4 SERVINGS

4 ounces wide rice noodles

1 cup mung bean sprouts

½ cup chicken stock or broth

1 teaspoon soy sauce

2 tablespoons oil for stir-frying

1 cup cooked beef, shredded

¼ teaspoon chili paste

2 tablespoons Burmese-Style Mustard Greens (see Part II)

1. Soak the rice noodles in hot water for at least 15 minutes to soften. Drain well. Blanch the mung bean sprouts by plunging briefly into boiling water. Drain well.

2. Combine the chicken broth and soy sauce. Set aside.

3. Add oil to a preheated wok or skillet. When oil is hot, add the noodles. Stir-fry briefly, then add the sauce. Mix with the noodles and add the shredded beef. Stir in the chili paste and the Burmese-Style Mustard Greens. Add the mung bean sprouts. Mix through and serve hot.

BARBECUE RIBS with RED ONION SAUCE

This is a method for making barbecued ribs in your oven instead of the grill so you can make them anytime of the year. Of course, you don't have to save your ribs (and your pickles) for the fall and winter. These ribs are just as delicious fired low and slow over indirect heat on a grill.

YIELDS 2 SERVINGS

2 tablespoons paprika

1 clove garlic, peeled and minced

2 teaspoons salt

1 teaspoon sugar

1 teaspoon pepper

1 teaspoon dried oregano

1 teaspoon dried thyme

1 slab baby back pork ribs

½ cup barbecue sauce

3 tablespoons Caramelized Red Onion Relish (see Part II)

1. Preheat oven to 350°F.
2. Mix dry ingredients together in a bowl, and then rub the mixture on both sides of the ribs. Place ribs in a roasting pan, cover, and bake for 2 hours.
3. Remove cooked ribs from oven. In a small bowl, mix together barbecue sauce and Caramelized Red Onion Relish. Brush on the barbecue sauce mixture, and bake uncovered for 10 minutes.
4. Cut slab in half to serve two.

BANH MI

Banh Mi are an example of the legacy left by the French on Vietnamese cuisine: crusty French rolls stuffed with pickled Asian vegetables. This is a great way to use up leftover roasted chicken, but you could use any filling you like, such as pork, shrimp, tofu, or even fried eggs.

YIELDS 4 SERVINGS

2 tablespoons canola oil

½ pound beef skirt steak or hanger steak, cut into thin strips

½ teaspoon salt

½ teaspoon pepper

¼ cup sliced white onion

4 crusty French rolls (or 1–2 baguettes sliced into 4 sandwich-length segments)

Mayonnaise, to taste

Soy sauce or Maggi seasoning

2 tablespoons Pungent Pickled Garlic (see Part II)

1 small cucumber, peeled and seeded and cut into spears

5 cilantro sprigs, roughly chopped

¼ cup Vegetable Medley (see Part II)

1. In a large skillet, heat the canola oil over medium heat until it begins to simmer.

2. Season the steak strips with salt and pepper, and then cook them in the skillet, tossing them frequently, until they've reached their desired degree of doneness (about 3–5 minutes for medium). Add the sliced onion to wilt momentarily, then remove the pan from the heat, and let cool.

3. Split French rolls and slather insides with mayonnaise. Add a few drops of soy sauce or Maggi, and spread some of the Pungent Pickled Garlic on each roll.

4. Stuff each sandwich with all of the fillings: steak, onions, cucumber spears, and cilantro. Add Vegetable Medley. Serve the sandwiches at room temperature.

TERIYAKI SALMON BURGERS with PICKLED CARROTS

These sweet salmon burgers are a quick and healthy dinner that can feed a crowd. The Pickled Carrots add a touch of refinement and elegance to this perfect weeknight dish.

YIELDS 4 SERVINGS

3 tablespoons soy sauce

½ cup water

½ cup pineapple juice

1 tablespoon diced Pickled Ginger (see Part II)

3 tablespoons brown sugar

1-pound salmon fillet, skin and bones removed

½ cup unflavored bread crumbs

½ teaspoon salt

¼ teaspoon pepper

Vegetable oil, for cooking

4 pita bread pockets

4 tablespoons Picked Carrots (see Part III)

Lettuce, tomato, and onion garnishes (optional)

1. In a medium saucepan, combine the first five ingredients, and bring to a low boil over medium heat. Once the mixture is boiling, set it aside briefly to cool, and then pour it into a glass baking dish. Add the salmon fillet to the marinade, and allow it to rest for up to two hours in the refrigerator, turning every 30 minutes.

2. After two hours, remove the salmon from the marinade and pat it dry. Process the salmon fillet in a food processor until well chopped.

3. In a large bowl, mix the chopped salmon with the breadcrumbs, and season with the salt and pepper.

4. Heat a cast iron pan or grill pan over medium high heat until hot, and add enough vegetable oil to lightly coat the bottom of the pan.

5. Cook the salmon burgers for approximately 3 minutes on each side, until a thermometer placed in the center of a burger reads at least 135°F.

6. Place each salmon burger into a pita pocket, and top each sandwich with an equal portion of Pickled Carrots. Add optional garnishes, if desired.

FISH TACOS with CORN RELISH

This is a more upscale recipe, typically served near Texas's Gulf Coast. You can certainly substitute breaded fish sticks for the fresh fish, but try it this way once.

YIELDS 4–6 SERVINGS

1 pound red snapper fillets

3 tablespoons cornmeal

1 tablespoon flour

½ teaspoon salt

2 teaspoons chili powder

¼ teaspoon cumin

¼ teaspoon pepper

1 egg, beaten

3 tablespoons heavy cream

3 tablespoons chopped cilantro

⅓ cup sour cream

¼ cup olive oil

1 avocado

1 tablespoon lime juice

8 crisp taco shells, heated

1 (15-ounce) can cannelloni beans, rinsed

2 cups shredded lettuce

1 cup shredded Monterey jack cheese

¼ cup Corn Relish (see Part II)

1. Cut fish fillets into 1-inch pieces and set aside. In shallow bowl, combine cornmeal, flour, salt, chili powder, cumin, and pepper and mix well. In another shallow bowl, combine egg and cream and beat until combined. Dip fish pieces into egg mixture, then roll in cornmeal mixture to coat; set on wire rack.

2. In small bowl, combine cilantro and sour cream; blend well, cover, and place in refrigerator. Heat olive oil in heavy skillet over medium heat. Cook coated fish pieces in oil for 3–4 minutes, turning once, until golden brown. Peel and dice avocado and sprinkle with lime juice. Add the beans and cook gently until warm.

3. Make tacos by filling heated taco shells with fish, beans, avocado, cilantro sauce, lettuce, and cheese. Top with Corn Relish before serving.

NEW ENGLAND BOILED DINNER

This is almost a period-style recipe, with classic tastes comple-mented by traditional Heirloom Pickles. Serve with Apple Crisp for dessert on a blustery fall day.

YIELDS 6 SERVINGS

3-pound corned beef brisket

6 medium carrots

3 medium potatoes

3 medium parsnips

6 small yellow onions

½ head medium-sized cabbage

1½ teaspoons whole black peppercorns

2 bay leaves

1½ cups 2% milk

4 teaspoons cornstarch

2 tablespoons horseradish mustard

¼ cup Heirloom Mustard Pickles (see Part II)

1. Trim excess fat from the meat. Peel the carrots and cut into chunks. Peel the potatoes and cut into quarters. Peel the parsnips and cut into chunks. Peel the onions and cut in half. Shred the cabbage.

2. Place the meat in a Dutch oven. Add the juices and spices from the package included with meat. Add enough water to cover the meat. Add the peppercorns and bay leaves. Bring to a boil. Reduce heat and simmer, covered, for 2 hours.

3. Add the carrots, potatoes, parsnips, and onions to the Dutch oven. Return to boiling. Reduce heat and simmer, covered, for 10 minutes. Add the cabbage and cook for 20 minutes or until the vegetables are tender

4. Remove the meat and vegetables from the liquid. Discard the liquid and bay leaves. Slice the meat across the grain.

5. Make the mustard sauce by stirring together the milk and cornstarch in a small saucepan. Cook over medium heat and stir until thickened and bubbly. Once bubbles start forming, turn down the heat to low, and cook and stir for 2 minutes more. Stir in the mustard, and then add the Heirloom Mustard Pickles. Heat through.

6. Put the meat and vegetables on a platter and drizzle with the mustard sauce.

PRIME RIB with QUICK-PICKLED RAMP AIOLI

This succulent roast is traditionally served with horseradish cream, which has been replaced in this quirky recipe with a powerful ramp aioli.

YIELDS 8 SERVINGS

18-pound boneless beef rib roast

2 tablespoons chopped fresh rosemary

¼ cup kosher salt

2 tablespoons cracked black pepper

4 cloves garlic, peeled

½ cup Pickled Ramps (see Part II)

¼ teaspoon salt

1 cup mayonnaise

1 teaspoon lemon juice

1 tablespoon olive oil

1. Preheat oven to 450°F.
2. Rub the outside of the roast with the rosemary, salt, and pepper, leaving a crust.
3. Mince the garlic and the Pickled Ramps, sprinkle them with the salt, and continue mincing. Turn the knife blade parallel to the cutting board and mash the vegetables and salt into a paste.
4. Put the paste in a bowl with the mayonnaise and whisk together. Add lemon juice and whisk again.
5. Pour oil in a stream while whisking it into the mayonnaise mixture. Once the oil is added, the aioli should be kept in the refrigerator until the dish is ready to come together.
6. Place the roast in a roasting pan and put it in the oven. Roast for 15 minutes.
7. Reduce the oven temperature to 325°F and continue to roast for 1½ hours. Check internal temperature with a meat thermometer; when it reaches 120°F, remove the roast from the oven. Let the roast stand, covered, for at least 15 minutes before carving to let the temperature rise and allow the juices to settle back into the meat.
8. Remove the aioli from the refrigerator and allow it to come back to room temperature.
9. Roast internal temperature will rise 10°F during the resting period after it is removed from the oven. Finished temperatures are 125°F for rare, 130°F for medium rare, and 135–145°F for medium. Serve the roast sliced and smothered with the aioli.

PAN-SEARED DUCK BREAST
with SHALLOTS

This is a time-intensive but extremely elegant dish, worthy of a special occasion. Duck has a special affinity for shallots and warming spices, the flavors of which are imparted deeply into the breast as it marinates. Additionally, the vinegar in the pickled shallots is reflected by the tart peach sauce that finishes the dish.

YIELDS 2 SERVINGS

1 boneless whole duck breast

4 cups Shallot Confiture (see Part II)

Salt and pepper

1 shallot, chopped

1 tablespoon butter

1 fresh peach, chopped with peel on

2 tablespoons rice vinegar

1 tablespoon amaretto liqueur

½ cup chicken broth

1. The day before you plan on cooking this dish, marinate the duck breast in the refrigerator in Shallot Confiture for 12 hours. When it's time to cook, wipe off the marinade.

2. Preheat oven to 375°F.

3. Score the skin on duck breast, season both sides with salt and pepper, and sear it, skin side down, in a sauté pan over medium-high heat for 3 minutes. Remove duck breast from sauté pan and place it, skin side up, in a baking dish. Put the duck in the oven to finish cooking for about 5 minutes.

4. In the same sauté pan, cook the shallots in butter for 2 minutes; add peach, vinegar, and amaretto.

5. Cook to reduce liquid by half. Add broth, and cook for 5 minutes more. Adjust seasoning with salt and pepper.

6. Slice the duck breast and fan the slices on a plate. Spoon the peach sauce over the meat.

GOAN CHICKEN CURRY

This delight from western India takes a bit of an effort to make, but the results are really rewarding. Feel free to use only one of the pickles listed here.

YIELDS 4–5 SERVINGS

1 tablespoon poppy seeds

1 tablespoon mustard seeds

2 teaspoons cumin seeds

1 tablespoon coriander seeds

1 teaspoon black peppercorns

1 cinnamon stick

1 tablespoon cloves

¼ cup unsweetened coconut

3 tablespoons vegetable oil

1 large red onion, diced

1½ pounds skinless boneless chicken, cut into chunks

2 teaspoons Pickled Ginger Sauce (see Part III)

2 tablespoons Indian Mixed Greens (see Part II)

1 15-ounce can lentils

Water, as needed

1 tablespoon lemon juice (optional)

1. In a small skillet on medium heat, dry roast the poppy seeds, mustard seeds, cumin seeds, coriander seeds, black peppercorns, cinnamon stick, and cloves. When the spices release their aroma, remove from heat and let cool. In a spice grinder, coffee grinder, or with a mortar and pestle, grind the spices, along with the coconut, to a coarse powder. Set aside.

2. In a large skillet, heat the vegetable oil. Add the onion and sauté until well browned, about 7–8 minutes.

3. Add the chicken and sauté until browned, about 5–7 minutes. Add the Pickled Ginger Sauce, the Indian Mixed Greens, the reserved spice powder, and the lentils, sauté for 2 minutes.

4. Add about ½ cup of water and bring to a boil. Reduce the heat, cover, and simmer until the chicken is cooked through, about 10 to 15 minutes. If the water evaporates, add more as necessary. Add 1 tablespoon of lemon juice to the dish before serving, if desired. Serve hot.

PORK CARNITAS

Carnitas are exceptionally tender and flavorful because of their long, slow roasting time. This particular recipe adds the salty, spicy punch of pickled peppers for a taste sensation that rivals the best taco stands in the country.

YIELDS 10–12 SERVINGS

1 (3-pound) pork shoulder roast

1 teaspoon salt

1 teaspoon pepper

2–3 tablespoons olive oil

1 thinly sliced onion

4 medium tomatoes

½ teaspoon dried oregano

1 teaspoon cumin powder

2 bay leaves

2 whole cloves

2 tablespoons chopped Salt-Cured Thai Chilies
    (see Part II)

¾ cup water or beef stock

1. Preheat the oven to 325°F. Salt and pepper the pork when you first remove it from the refrigerator. Then allow the pork to come to room temperature for approximately 45 minutes to 1 hour. This will give the seasonings time to penetrate the meat.

2. Preheat the oven to 325°F.

3. Add olive oil to a large ovenproof pan, and sear the pork in the pan over medium-high heat for 5 minutes per side. Make sure not to turn the pork too soon, or you'll inhibit the development of a good, brown crust.

4. After you've thoroughly browned the pork, remove it from the pan and let it rest for 10–15 minutes.

5. While the pan is still hot, add the onion slices and cook over low heat for 2–3 minutes until translucent. Return the pork to the pan and add the remaining ingredients in the pan around the pork.

6. Cover and place in the oven. Cook for 2–3 hours, until the internal temperature reaches 140°F–150°F. Let the roast rest for 10–15 minutes before slicing.

MAPO DOFU with KIMCHI

This dish is traditionally served with ground Sichuan peppercorns for its spice component, but here we've substituted some fiery kimchi for a slightly different take on a hip yet classic meatless entrée.

YIELDS 4 SERVINGS

¾ **pound firm tofu**

½ **pound ground pork**

4 **tablespoons soy sauce, divided**

1½ **teaspoons sugar, divided**

1½ **teaspoons cornstarch**

2 **stalks bok choy with leaves**

1 **green onion, chopped**

⅔ **cup chicken broth**

⅓ **cup water**

1 **teaspoon Chinese rice wine or dry sherry**

½ **teaspoon sesame oil**

2 **tablespoons oil for stir-frying**

2 **slices ginger, minced**

2 **garlic cloves, peeled and minced**

¼ **teaspoon chili paste**

2 **teaspoons cornstarch**

4 **teaspoons water**

2 **tablespoons Hot and Pungent Kimchi (see Part II)**

1. Drain the tofu and cut into ½-inch cubes.

2. Place ground pork in a medium bowl. Add 2 tablespoons soy sauce and ½ teaspoon sugar. Then add 1½ teaspoons cornstarch. Marinate the pork for 30 minutes.

3. Wash the bok choy and drain thoroughly. Separate the stalks and leaves. Cut into 1-inch pieces.

4. Chop the green onion into 1-inch pieces.

5. Combine the chicken broth, water, 2 tablespoons soy sauce, 1 teaspoon sugar, rice wine, and sesame oil.

6. Add oil to a preheated wok or skillet. When oil is hot, add the ginger, garlic, green onion, and chili paste, and stir-fry until aromatic. Add the ground pork. Cook until it changes color, then push up to the side and add the bok choy. Stir-fry 3–5 minutes.

7. In a small bowl, combine the cornstarch and water.

8. Add the chicken broth/soy sauce mixture to the middle of the wok and bring to a boil. Give the cornstarch-and-water mixture a quick stir and add to the sauce, stirring quickly to thicken. Turn down the heat slightly and add the tofu. Add the Hot and Pungent Kimchi. Mix everything through and cook for 5 more minutes. Serve hot.

SKEWERED LEMONGRASS CHICKEN

These deceptively delicious chicken skewers are an excellent main course for a summer party. The deep and pungent flavors, combined with the caramelization from the high heat of the grill, make for a taste that will be remembered!

YIELDS 4 SERVINGS

5 stalks lemongrass, trimmed

2 pounds skinless chicken breasts, cut into cubes

Black pepper

2 tablespoons vegetable oil, divided

Pinch of dried red pepper flakes

2 tablespoons Green Coriander Chutney (see Part II)

Juice of 1 lime

2 teaspoons fish sauce

Pinch of sugar

Sea salt to taste

Limes for garnish

1. Remove and discard 2 inches from the thick end of each stalk of lemongrass. Bruise 4 of the lemongrass stalks with the back of a knife. Remove the tough outer layer of the fifth stalk, exposing the tender core; mince.

2. Skewer 3 cubes of chicken on each lemongrass stalk. Sprinkle the skewers with the minced lemongrass and black pepper, and drizzle with 1 tablespoon of oil. Cover with plastic wrap and refrigerate for 12 to 24 hours.

3. Chop all of the reserved lemongrass stalk ends. Place in a small saucepan and cover with water. Bring to a boil, cover, and let reduce until approximately 2 tablespoons of liquid is left; strain. Return the liquid to the saucepan and further reduce to 1 tablespoon.

4. Combine the lemongrass liquid with the red pepper flakes, Green Coriander Chutney, lime juice, fish sauce, sugar, and remaining tablespoon of oil; set aside.

5. Prepare a grill to high heat. Brush both sides of the chicken with a little of the lemongrass sauce. Grill the chicken skewers for approximately 2 to 3 minutes per side, or until done to your liking.

6. To serve, sprinkle the chicken skewers with sea salt, and pass them with cut limes.

PORK in PLUM SAUCE

The sauce in this recipe is created by thinning out pickled plums with water to replicate a Chinese-style plum sauce with added bite.

YIELDS 4 SERVINGS

1 pound boneless pork loin chops

1 tablespoon soy sauce

1 tablespoon cornstarch

1 teaspoon baking soda

3 tablespoons oil for stir-frying

2 slices ginger

2 carrots, cut into matchsticks

½ cup Quick-Pickled Plums (see Part II)

½ cup water

2 green onions, thinly sliced on the diagonal

Pinch of fresh parsley, for garnish

1. Cut the pork into cubes and place into a large bowl. Add the soy sauce, cornstarch, and baking soda. Marinate the pork in the refrigerator for 90 minutes.
2. Add 2 tablespoons oil to a preheated wok or skillet. When oil is hot, add the pork. Stir-fry until it changes color and is nearly cooked through. Remove from the wok and drain on paper towels.
3. Add 1 tablespoon oil. When oil is hot, add the ginger slices and stir-fry briefly until aromatic. Add the carrots and stir-fry for about 1 minute.
4. Combine the Quick-Pickled Plums and the water to thin out their consistency. Add to the stir-fry.
5. Add the cooked pork. Stir in the green onions. Mix everything through, top the dish with parsley leaves, and serve hot.

PART IV

DRINKS WITH PICKLES

By now, you know how to incorporate your pickles into delicious condiments, starters, and even full entrees, but the true connoisseur can go even further! Any modern bar worth it's salt now has pickle-based cocktails on the menu, and with good reason—the intense flavor of preserved produce is one of the few things that can stand up to and fully complement alcohol. Whether the drinks are sweet, like Mango Chutney Margaritas, or intensely hot like the Prairie Fire Shooter, you'll find that pickles perk up run-of-the-mill drinks and add a unique air of modern class. Improvisation is key, so don't be afraid to go out of the box—you might just find that these are some of the best cocktails you'll ever try!

Caipiroska, see Part IV

BLOODY MARY

Pungent pickled peppers are a natural fit in this classic savory drink recipe.

YIELDS 1 SERVING

1½ ounces vodka

½ cup tomato juice

2 teaspoons lemon juice

Dash Tabasco sauce

1 ounce Worcestershire Sauce

1 cup ice

½ ounce pickle brine from Vinegar-Packed Peppers (see Part II)

Celery stick, lemon wedge, and Vinegar-Packed Pepper for garnish

Combine first seven ingredients in a cocktail shaker and shake well. Strain into a tall glass filled with ice cubes. Garnish and serve.

GARLIC GIBSON

The classic Gibson is defined by its iconic cocktail onion, but this daring derivative changes out the onion for a pickled garlic clove, for a novel twist on an old-fashioned favorite.

YIELDS 1 SERVING

1½ ounces dry gin

½ ounce French vermouth

3 cloves garlic from Pungent Pickled Garlic (see Part II)

1 lemon twist

Shake gin and vermouth in a shaker tin of ice. Strain into a martini glass. Garnish with Pungent Pickled Garlic and a lemon twist.

BULL SHOT

This hearty cocktail uses beef bouillon to achieve a body that you're not likely to find in any other drink.

YIELDS 1 SERVING

1½ ounces vodka

4 ounces chilled beef bouillon

Dash Worcestershire sauce, salt, and pepper

Rum Chilies (see Part II), for garnish

Combine ingredients in a shaker half-filled with ice. Shake well. Strain into a highball glass over ice. Garnish with Rum Chilies.

BLOODY CAESAR

This relative of the famous Bloody Mary is blasted past traditional with the addition of Clamato and pickled capers. Don't serve it to an unsuspecting friend!

YIELDS 1 SERVING

1½ ounes vodka

¼ ounce fresh lime juice

Clamato juice to fill

Celery salt, pepper, Tabasco sauce,
    Worcestershire sauce to taste

4–5 Brined Capers (see Part II)

Combine all liquid ingredients and spices with ice and stir. Strain into a tall glass filled with ice. Garnish with Brined Capers.

Is Clamato What It Sounds Like?

Clamato is indeed a mixture made from clam and tomato juice! It's got a unique flavor that pairs exceptionally well with drinks like the Bloody Caesar and Bloody Mary, but it's not for the uninitiated.

CAIPIROSKA

Caipiroska is a popular lime and vodka drink that is especially prevalent in South America. One taste of this, and you're in the tropics!

YIELDS 1 SERVING

¼ **lime**

1 Pickled Lime quarter (see Part II)

2 teaspoons sugar

2 ounces vodka

1 cup ice

Muddle the limes and sugar in a mixing glass. Add the vodka and ice. Shake, then strain into a rocks glass of cracked ice.

Drink It Raw!

To make this drink most reminiscent of its birthplace, use raw or turbinado sugar as the sweetener here instead of processed white sugar.

HAIRY NAVEL

This peach-based cocktail is complemented well by a pickled peach garnish. The sweetness of the orange juice in the drink is offset by the pungent and nuanced taste of the peach.

YIELDS 1 SERVING

1 ounce vodka

1 ounce peach schnapps

Fresh orange juice to fill

1 slice Pickled Peaches (see Part II)

Pour the vodka and peach schnapps into a highball glass of ice. Fill with orange juice. Garnish with the Pickled Peach slice.

BORDEN CHASE with ORANGE RIND

This is a serious connoisseur's drink featuring Scotch, vermouth, absinthe, and hints of orange.

YIELDS 1 SERVING

2 ounces Scotch

½ ounce dry vermouth

¼ ounce absinthe

2 dashes orange bitters

Spiced Orange Rings (see Part II), for garnish

Shake all the ingredients in a shaker tin with ice. Then strain into a chilled martini glass. Garnish with the orange rings.

PICKLED GEORGIA PEACH

This delightful drink is a pure glass of the South. It's incredibly refreshing on a hot and humid summer day.

YIELDS 1 SERVING

1½ ounces peach vodka

1 ounce peach-flavored brandy

¼ ounce lemon juice

1 teaspoon Pickled Peaches (see Part II)

½ fresh peach, cut up and peeled

½ cup ice

Combine ingredients in a blender with ice. Blend thoroughly. Pour into a tall glass.

The BEE'S KNEES

This cute-sounding recipe plays on the soothing combination of lemon and honey to create a smooth and comforting drink with a heavy dose of sweetness. The pickled lemon juice helps to offset the honey.

YIELDS 1 SERVING

2 ounces gin

¾ ounce honey

½ ounce fresh lemon juice

Dash juice from Preserved Lemons (see Part II)

Rind from Preserved Lemons (see Part II), for garnish

Shake all ingredients in a shaker tin of ice. Strain into a martini glass. Garnish with a pickled rind.

Amazing Antiseptics!

Every ingredient in this drink, from the honey to the pickled lemon juice, has antiseptic or antibiotic properties. Give it a try if you're feeling under the weather. Just don't drink too many servings!

WATERMELON COSMO

This drink lends itself well to a variety of pickled ingredients. We've recommended pairing it with Watermelon Pickles, but you could just as easily garnish it with Preserved Lemons or Spiced Orange Rings (see Part II) to play on the other flavors.

YIELDS 1 SERVING

1½ ounces watermelon vodka

½ ounce Cointreau

¼ ounce lime juice or freshly squeezed lime

1 ounce cranberry juice

Rind from Watermelon Pickles (see Part II)

Pour all liquid ingredients into a shaker tin of ice. Shake and strain into a martini glass. Garnish with the rind from Watermelon Pickles.

The BLUE MOON

Don't confuse this with the beer of a similar name! The Blue Moon is a lemon-flavored drink that gets playful with violet liqueur, an unusual floral note.

YIELDS 1 SERVING

2 ounces gin

1 ounce violet liqueur

½ ounce fresh lemon juice

1 piece lemon rind from Preserved Lemons (see Part II)

Shake all the liquid ingredients in a shaker tin with ice. Then strain into a chilled martini glass. Garnish with the preserved rind.

The Elusive Violet

Violet liqueur can be a bit difficult to obtain. If you can't find it, consider substituting it with a vanilla liqueur. If you do so, you might wish to add a small dash of pickled lemon juice to the cocktail to help cut through some of the pronounced vanilla sweetness.

CUCUMBER GIMLET with PICKLED LIME

This gimlet features the addition of cucumber to the normal gin and lime juice combination. The cucumber adds a lovely cooling touch to the already refreshing drink.

YIELDS 1 SERVING

2 tablespoons cucumber, chopped and
    de-seeded

2 ounces gin

½ ounce lime juice

½ ounce juice from Pickled Limes (see Part II)

1 ounce simple syrup

Drop the fresh cucumber into the bottom of a short glass and muddle. Add a handful of ice and the rest of the ingredients. Stir.

Really Should Be Rose's

For the nonpickled lime juice in this recipe, many purists consider Rose's lime juice to be the only acceptable or "real" version of this recipe. Of course, a purist likely wouldn't be drinking a pickled gimlet, so feel free to use fresh lime juice if that suits you.

MANGO CHUTNEY
MARGARITA

This is a creative blended margarita that picks up a number of unique flavors from the chutney, including the complementary taste of tropical mango!

YIELDS 1 SERVING

1½ ounces aged tequila

½ ounce triple sec

3 ounces margarita mix

1 tablespoon Mango Chutney (see Part II)

1 cup ice

Lime wheel for garnish

Put the first five ingredients in a blender and blend. Pour into a margarita glass and garnish with the lime wheel.

PICKLED DARK and STORMY

This deeply flavored cocktail gets two different pickled ingredients that act as a counterpoint to the heavy rum and ginger beer. If that's too much pickle for you, feel free to remove one of them.

YIELDS 1 SERVING

2 ounces Gosling's dark rum

Ginger beer to fill

Dash of liquid from Pickled Ginger (see Part II)

Dash of liquid from Pickled Limes (see Part II)

Rind from Pickled Limes (see Part II)

Pour the rum over ice in a highball glass and fill with ginger beer. Add the pickling liquids and garnish with the lime rind.

GIN-GIN MULE

Mint and ginger combine for a winning combination here. Pickled ginger juice is sweeter and much less salty than other pickle juices, so it won't disrupt the overall composition of this drink.

YIELDS 1 SERVING

1½ ounces gin

¾ ounce fresh lime juice

1 ounce simple syrup

6 sprigs fresh mint

1 ounce ginger beer

Dash of liquid from Pickled Ginger (see Part II)

Put the first four ingredients into a shaker tin of ice. Shake hard and strain into a highball glass of fresh ice. Top with ginger beer and the pickling liquid.

PRAIRIE FIRE SHOOTER

One taste and you'll understand why they call it fire. This is a hot-sauce shot that's made even better by the addition of spicy pickling liquid!

YIELDS 1 SERVING

1½ ounces tequila

2 dashes Tabasco

Dash of liquid from Vinegar-Packed Peppers (see Part II)

Pour tequila into a shot glass and add the Tabasco and pickling liquid.

Pickled Peppers and Hot Sauce

Pickled hot peppers are surprisingly very similar in taste to your favorite hot sauces. All of the same basic ingredients are there—chilies, vinegar, salt, seasonings—just arranged slightly differently.

KNOCK on WOOD with PEACH

This sophisticated Scotch drink is smooth and fruity. It's wonderful as an after-dinner cocktail.

YIELDS 1 SERVING

1½ ounces gin

2 ounces Scotch

½ ounce peach schnapps

½ ounce Madeira

2 dashes peach bitters

1 dash liquid from Pickled Peaches (see Part II)

Shake all the ingredients with ice and strain into a short glass of ice.

PICKLEBACK SHOT

This is the simplest and possibly the most effective of all pickle drink recipes. It may sound distasteful, but this drink has quite a following. The interplay of the whiskey and the salty brine is actually delicious.

YIELDS 1 SERVING

1½–2 ounces whiskey

1½–2 ounces liquid from Dill Pickles (see Part II)

Pour the whiskey into one shot glass, and the pickling liquid into another. Take the shot of whiskey and follow it immediately with the pickle shot.

DIRTY PICKLETINI

This drink takes the ultimate dirty cocktail and roughs it up some more, using pickle brine in place of the olive juice. The sour, salty cocktail takes the concept of dirty to the next level!

YIELDS 1 SERVING

2 ounces London dry gin
½ ounce pickle brine, from Dill Pickles (see Part II)
Olives for garnish

Shake liquid ingredients in a shaker tin of ice. Strain into a martini glass. Garnish with olives.

VODKA PICKLET

Cucumber pickles and citrus fruit? Surprisingly, this is an exceptional pairing. The acidity in the citrus is mirrored and complemented by the acidity in the brine for one stellar cocktail.

YIELDS 1 SERVING

1½ ounces vodka
½ ounce Rose's lime juice (or ¼ ounce fresh lime juice and ¼ ounce simple syrup)
½ ounce pickle brine from Dill Pickles (see Part II)
1 lime wedge, for garnish
2 pickle slices, for garnish

Add all liquid ingredients to a mixing glass half filled with ice. Shake and strain into a rocks glass of ice. Garnish with lime wedge and pickle slices.

Index

Standard U.S./Metric Measurement Conversions

VOLUME CONVERSIONS

U.S. Volume Measure	Metric Equivalent
⅛ teaspoon	0.5 milliliters
¼ teaspoon	1 milliliters
½ teaspoon	2 milliliters
1 teaspoon	5 milliliters
½ tablespoon	7 milliliters
1 tablespoon (3 teaspoons)	15 milliliters
2 tablespoons (1 fluid ounce)	30 milliliters
¼ cup (4 tablespoons)	60 milliliters
⅓ cup	90 milliliters
½ cup (4 fluid ounces)	125 milliliters
⅔ cup	160 milliliters
¾ cup (6 fluid ounces)	180 milliliters
1 cup (16 tablespoons)	250 milliliters
1 pint (2 cups)	500 milliliters
1 quart (4 cups)	1 liter (about)

WEIGHT CONVERSIONS

U.S. Weight Measure	Metric Equivalent
½ ounce	15 grams
1 ounce	30 grams
2 ounces	60 grams
3 ounces	85 grams
¼ pound (4 ounces)	115 grams
½ pound (8 ounces)	225 grams
¾ pound (12 ounces)	340 grams
1 pound (16 ounces)	454 grams

OVEN TEMPERATURE CONVERSIONS

Degrees Fahrenheit	Degrees Celsius
200 degrees F	95 degrees C
250 degrees F	120 degrees C
275 degrees F	135 degrees C
300 degrees F	150 degrees C
325 degrees F	160 degrees C
350 degrees F	180 degrees C
375 degrees F	190 degrees C
400 degrees F	205 degrees C
425 degrees F	220 degrees C
450 degrees F	230 degrees C

BAKING PAN SIZES

American	Metric
8 x 1½ inch round baking pan	20 x 4 cm cake tin
9 x 1½ inch round baking pan	23 x 3.5 cm cake tin
11 x 7 x 1½ inch baking pan	28 x 18 x 4 cm baking tin
13 x 9 x 2 inch baking pan	30 x 20 x 5 cm baking tin
2 quart rectangular baking dish	30 x 20 x 3 cm baking tin
15 x 10 x 2 inch baking pan	30 x 25 x 2 cm baking tin (Swiss roll tin)
9 inch pie plate	22 x 4 or 23 x 4 cm pie plate
7 or 8 inch springform pan	18 or 20 cm springform or loose bottom cake tin
9 x 5 x 3 inch loaf pan	23 x 13 x 7 cm or 2 lb narrow loaf or pate tin
1½ quart casserole	1.5 liter casserole
2 quart casserole	2 liter casserole

CONTAINS MATERIAL ADAPTED AND ABRIDGED FROM: